Moving Bodies, Navigating Conflict

Practicing
Bharata Natyam
in Colombo,
Sri Lanka

**Ahalya
Satkunaratnam**

WESLEYAN UNIVERSITY PRESS

Middletown, Connecticut

Moving
Bodies,
Navigating
Conflict

Wesleyan University Press
Middletown, CT 06459
www.wesleyan.edu/wespress
© 2020 Ahalya Satkunaratnam
All rights reserved
Manufactured in the United States of America
Designed by Richard Hendel
Typeset in Chaparral and Bunday Sans
by Tseng Information Systems, Inc.

Library of Congress Cataloging-in-Publication Data
available upon request

Hardcover ISBN: 978-0-8195-7889-1
Paperback ISBN: 978-0-8195-7890-7
Ebook ISBN: 978-0-8195-7891-4

5 4 3 2 1

To the artists and cultural workers who imagine for us

Contents

Acknowledgments

This book is a project that is written through connection, mentorship, and immense generosity. Thanks go to all the artists, cultural workers, teachers, and families who spoke with me and assisted my own navigation of research, writing, and living in Colombo. Thank you for giving me your time and your wisdom and opening your homes to me (and continuing to do so). Your friendship and support created this book and transformed me on the way.

There are many teachers who have guided me to this place: Hema Rajagopalan, S. Rajeswari, Kamala Kumar, Vasanthi Iyer, Dr. Gnana Kulendran, Arunthathy Sri Padmanathan, Sivakumari Gnanendran, Daya Mahinda, and Lakshmi Sriharan. This research benefited from the 2012–14 Andrew. W. Mellon Postdoctoral Fellowship in the Humanities through the Illinois Program for Research in the Humanities (IPRH) at the University of Illinois and Urbana-Champaign. I thank IPRH, the Department of Gender and Women's Studies, and the Department of Dance at UIUC for providing me a rigorous and intellectual community for two years. Special thanks goes to Mimi T. Nguyen for continued support and inspiration. Thank yous go to Laurie Fuller, Ann Russo, and Gabriel Cortez for opportunities and mentorship when I first returned to Chicago. Thanks go to the Department of Dance at University of California–Riverside and to my doctoral dissertation committee, who supported my journey over the years: Priya Srinivasan, Anthea Kraut, Sally Ness, and Josh Kun. This project was also made possible through the generous support of the American Institute for Sri Lankan Studies Fellowship, the U.S. Department of Education Fulbright-Hays Doctoral Dissertation Research Award, and gifts and grants from the American Institute for Indian Studies, University of California, Riverside, and University of California, Berkeley.

Phil Friedrich, Sheetal Chhabria, and Sujatha Meegama provided insights on drafts of this work at many different stages in the writing. Vivimarie Vanderpoorten, Niruba Pushparaj, Uditha Senaratne, and Michael Meyler provided a rich, intellectual, and caring community over my many visits to Colombo. Thanks go to fellow students at University of California—Joti Singh, Shakina Nayfack, Alison Bory, and Mark Broomfield—for reading, writing, and dancing. I must also thank Umang Sharma, Shilpa Bavikatte, Sabba Elahi, and Kay Fujiyoshi for keeping in touch across place and time. My colleague Curtis Wasson graciously read over this work too. I thank Bianca Brigidi, Ellen Flournoy, Fei Shi, Seema Mehra, and Cynthia Patton for continued solidarities. Students, in particular, my mentees at Quest University Canada, brought me so much joy these past years; they were immensely supportive in the final months of writing. I am indebted to the committed education and dancing communities in Chicago and in the Bay Area.

I also would like to acknowledge that this book was completed on the traditional, ancestral, and unceded lands of the Squamish, Tseil-Waututh, and Musqueum Nations. I am humbled to have visited this land and to have learned from it during this life's journey. I also wish to acknowledge the many indigenous territories and peoples across what we call South Asia and Southeast Asia that have provided me rest and respite in times of dispossession and violent discrimination.

Transnational feminist scholarship, "third world" feminist discourse, and postcolonial theory across Sri Lanka, South Asia, and the United States have given me direction and have influenced the work in this book. I thank these scholars for their words and work. I also thank Susan Reed for her research and guidance since the beginnings of this project.

Wesleyan University Press and Suzanna Tamminen supported this work from the beginning. I thank Susan Silver for copyediting the text with detailed attention and managing editor Mary Garrett for assisting me with the final steps. Thank you also goes to the four anonymous readers who provided helpful and insightful comments that provided me with space to push this book further. An earlier version of "Staging War" appeared in *Dance Research Journal* 45, no. 1 (2013): 81–110.

Finally, I offer my gratitude to my mother and father, Pushpa and Satku; my brother, Abheha; and my nephews, Vivek and Arjun. I am indebted to my cousins, Vicknesh and Sumitha, for first steps and to my extensive family in Malaysia for the sweetest care. I am ever grateful to my dancing aunties and cousins for always providing me with inspiration. I thank the Divine and Ultimate Force.

Moving Bodies, Navigating Conflict

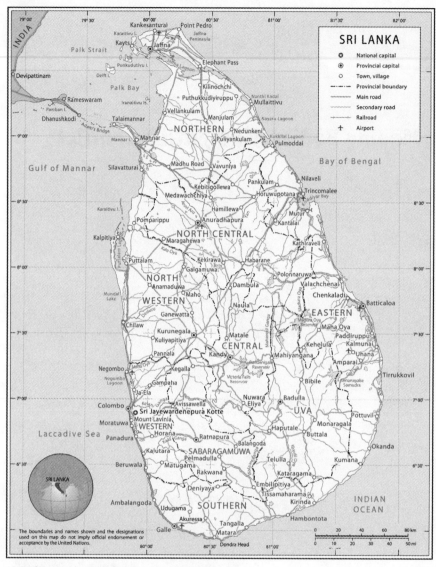

Map of Sri Lanka, 2008. Department of Field Support,
Geospatial Information Section, United Nations.

Introduction
Maneuvering Identity, Shifting Nations

Dressed in matching costumes of blue, red, and gold and decked in similarly hued jewels, a group of female *bharata natyam* dancers silently assemble themselves in rows on the dimly lit stage. Behind them lies a brightly colored panel of religious architecture: a minaret of a mosque, a stupa of a Buddhist temple, a *gopuram* or tower of a Hindu temple, and a steeple of a Christian church. A common and familiar Carnatic invocatory song rushes through the speakers to fill the auditorium.[1] "Gaja Vadana," in praise of Lord Ganesha, describes him as the elephant-faced lord full of love and compassion for his devotees.[2] In unison the dancers trace with their left hands the shape of an elephant trunk; their hands glide from their faces toward their waists, only to sway upward again. Fanning back and forth, their right hands in the tightly held *ardha chandra* mudra form elephant ears, while their legs bend deeply in *aramandi* as their torsos oscillate from side to side.[3] The female dancers interpret the accompanying lyrics with delicate hand movements and emphatic facial expressions. They convey the kindness of Ganesha as their fingertips "blossom" from closed buds to open flowers in the *alapadma* mudra flowing from their hearts.[4] Their eyebrows flicker up and down as their eyes fill with admiration of Ganesha's beautiful form. Unexpectedly, the music shifts from the Carnatic song to the popular melody of "Gajaga Vannam," with high-pitched trumpet sounds that typically accompany Buddhist *peraheras*, or processions.[5] With this musical shift, the dancers widen their stance. They undulate from side to side with their arms outstretched from their shoulders. Their hands turn gracefully, facing in and out. As they pivot back on their left foot, their right foot steps heavily, rotating their bodies into a spin.

Sitting in the audience, I notice supportive smiles and applause in appreciation of the acumen of the female bharata natyam dancers in portraying two distinct dance techniques. The choreography synchronously showcases commonalities between the two dance forms through the sways of torsos, the tracing of circular shapes with extended arms, and the grandeur of the lift and fall of flattened feet. The movements evoke the common admiration of the elephant in spiritual spaces and hints at the mutual faith in Ganesha, Pillaiyar, or Vinayakar among both Sinhala Buddhists and Tamil Hindus of Sri Lanka.[6] This audience and these young female bharata natyam dancers have assembled in a neighborhood hall of Bambalapitya, Colombo, for an interfaith service. Yet beyond these walls Colombo is marked with an expansive network of military checkpoints; routine, middle-of-the-night searches in "suspicious" neighborhoods; and frequent disappearances. War between the Sinhala-Buddhist government of Sri Lanka and the Tamil separatists, the Liberation Tigers of Tamil Eelam, is escalating to what will be—unbeknownst to anyone at the time—the final phase of the twenty-six-year war.[7] As bodies, specifically Tamil bodies, are subject to patrols, exclusion, and subjection on the streets of Colombo, dancing bodies maneuver through obstructions and hurdles both onstage and off.

The hybrid *Gaja Vadana/Gajaga Vannam* performed by bharata natyam dancers ask us to consider the politicizing of movement, bodies, and culture through conflict. It invites us to query the relationship between dances within a militarized nation: Kandyan dance, considered a representative of the Sinhala nation-state, and bharata natyam, a global form embraced by dancers across ethnic and national lines but simultaneously accepted as Tamil. The juxtaposition of the forms suggests a desire among this audience, dancers, and dance teacher for movement across boundaries of culture and ethnicity. It also provokes an inquiry into such traversals managed in the space and time of war, where bodies are denied identification beyond the limits imposed by ethnic categories defined by family names, native tongues, and village homes. The intersections of embodied, cultural practice and war demands an analysis of the imaginative, material, and discursive navigations of identities and their representations—often confined in service of advancing nationalism. This is the story of *Moving Bodies, Navigating Conflict: Practicing Bharata Natyam in Colombo, Sri Lanka.*

Moving Bodies, Navigating Conflict examines the relationships between aesthetics, embodied forms, and political work; the intersections of gender and sexuality with cultural practice and ethnic identity; and the experience of war and militarism in Sri Lanka documented through ethnographic practice. War transforms physical, emotional, and social landscapes (Thiranagama 2011). Dance evokes, converges with, and embodies these transformations. War charges dance with additional value, as specific cultural representations are desired by forces of nationalism and conflict—a means for demonstrating territorial domains on specific stages. Yet dance practice can also become a vehicle for the individual to resist such claims on the body, geographies, and the state. Through this highly codified form of bharata natyam, a form widely accepted as tradition and not suspect of contemporary creativity or present-day political resistance, dancers can insert their own desires. During war, dancing bodies navigate both histories of conflict and manage the contemporary, material, and ideological terrain of political nationalism. To fully comprehend the significance of dance and dancing during war, material and ideological terrains need to meet subjective terrains of experience.

Ethnicity and Militarism in Sri Lanka

The war that engulfed the nation for twenty-six years occurred between actors "who lived in the same local worlds" (Das and Kleinman 2000, 1). A "hybrid island," to borrow from Neluka Silva (2002), Sri Lanka is diverse in terms of ethnicity, language, and religion. The island nation, located fifty miles off the southeastern coast of India and in the Indian Ocean, has been a hub of mixture and migration, occupation, and colonization.[8] This text is about the construction of ethnicity and the ways in which it is embodied—materially and rhetorically and through performance; identity is central to the constructions of the civil war.

As Sharika Thiranagama so eloquently summarizes, Sri Lanka is split in terms of language between Tamil and Sinhala speakers, but these two languages are spoken across religion and ethnicity and yet are inscribed onto identity, subsequently framing the popular understandings of the ethnic conflict as one between Tamils and the Sinhala people (2011, 12). The largest community in terms of ethnicity are the Sinhala who speak Sinhala, of whom the majority are Theravada Buddhist, the minority of whom practice various dominations of Christianity. Tamil speakers are composed of different ethnic groups. The Sri Lankan Tamils are the largest Tamil-speaking minority group and are central to the ethnic conflict. The second largest minority are the Muslims. Although Tamil-speaking, Muslims are identified by the categories of religion and ethnicity. Sri Lankan Tamils are composed of Hindus and Christians and are classified by the categories of language and ethnicity. As Thiranagama states, "There are many other minorities who speak Sinhala, Tamil, or English," such as the Wanniya Laeto (indigenous peoples), Portuguese, and Dutch Burghers, "but they are not involved in the ethnic conflict on grounds of language or ethnicity." Ethnic communities have lived in various parts of the island, but the concentration of Tamils and Muslims in the north and east created the foundation for a separatist claim.[9] The third-most significant Tamil-speaking minority are the Malaiyaha Tamils, who are descendants of South Indian plantation labor brought by the British (2011, 13). As discussed in chapter 1 of this book, the Malaiyaha Tamils have suffered intense discrimination and continue to face marginalization.

Although one can speak of ethnic composition across the island this way, there is still complexity within and among ethnicity. Tamils identify regionally as well: East Coast (from Batticaloa and Trincomalee), Jaffna, and Northern (Vanni). Caste and class also further subdivide communities. And there are many divisions within ethnic communities that oppose war and the political leadership often "assigned" to their respective groups.

As with many ethnic conflicts, one body cannot be distinguished from another through physical, visible markers. Sameness is determined through the ambiguous notion of cultural identification—a Mobius strip that circles, folds, and twists ways of life and forms of signification—including, in part, language. This is most clearly demonstrated in the retellings of the many riots and pogroms that marked the history of the nation: oncoming mobs would ask their prospective victims to speak their language to determine whether they were the Other or not (Jeganathan 2003, 146). The Other is not apparent, but performance—desired, demanded—confirms its presence.

Getting at the ontology of identification and its transposition onto ethnicity or state belonging or rejection is not the intention of this project, but the ways in which identity is performed and negotiated to access political power is. I am indebted to the interdisciplinary work of Sri Lankan studies scholars who have excellently illuminated the construction of ethnicity in Sri Lanka and discussed the complex politics of the country. Neil DeVotta (2000, 2004) and A. Jeyaratnam Wilson (2000) discuss how racial labels were assigned to language practices. The Sinhala language was accepted as a descendant of Sanskrit and Pali, thus Aryan, while the Tamil language was labeled as Dravidian. These two authors also discuss how the British Empire contributed to differences between the Tamils and the Sinhala, assigning different jobs and positions to each community within the colonial state, in essence, reifying difference in class and power during imperial rule. But, as Thiranagama states, "The British did not 'invent' ethnicity in Sri Lanka"; however, the ways in which they made sense of the island's social and religious heterogeneity was through "popular Victorian ideas of race, linking this to religion and language differences," which became more "solid and 'ethnic'" when they were linked to political structures (2011, 21).[10]

The performance of ethnicity, held significant in the colonial era, was magnified in the postcolonial period. The island achieved independence from Britain in 1948, and ethnically marked political parties struggled over power, some committed to nonviolence, others to armed struggle; some fostered nationalism and communalism within their constituencies, and others rejected such notions (Jayawardena and de Alwis 1996).[11] Ancient texts that describe primeval warring between rulers constructed as representatives of the contemporary Sinhala and Tamil people were selectively recalled by nationalists and entwined with the emerging conflict. These acts transferred to arguments of Sinhala indigeneity and rights to nation and the subsequent labeling of Tamils as foreigners. The emerging Sinhala-nationalist agenda progressively disenfranchised Tamils from opportunities in education and employment and from claims of belonging as land was actively settled in the postindependence era.

Several groups, both nonviolent and armed, would compete to represent the minority Tamil cause. By the early 1980s the Liberation Tigers of Tamil Eelam, also known as the Tamil Tigers, forcefully established themselves as representatives. The Tigers—in pursuit of a separate Tamil homeland, Tamil Eelam—and the government of Sri Lanka would engage in armed conflict marked by direct combat, irregular eruptions of violence in noncombat zones, and periods of tension marked by escalations of surveillance. The postcolonial nation, and the war that emerged within it, was accompanied by a surge of international intervention in the form of aid and development by governmental and nongovernmental campaigns. A Norway-brokered Cease-Fire Agreement was signed in 2002, but hostilities resurfaced in 2005. By 2007—the year that marks the beginning of this ethnographic work— the government and Tigers entered what would be recognized, in retrospect, the final phase of the war (Bose 2007, 53–54). The war was declared over in May 2009 with the killing of the leadership of the Liberation Tigers of Tamil Eelam, but it has been argued that both the LTTE and the Sri Lanka armed forces caused severe civilian causalities (Ethirajan 2009; "Sri Lanka Says" 2009).

War produces notions of home and belonging locally, nationally, and globally. Geographies become more segregated with war and its many apparatuses of combat—riots, intimidation, roadblocks, disappearances, and checkpoints. Homes, streets, towns, and nations became marked (by ethnicity and religion) and transformed into objects in need of defense (from intrusion and mixing). Over the duration of the war, tens of thousands were killed, several thousand went missing, and a diaspora of hundreds of thousands was created through those who sought refuge in Europe, North America, India, and Australia (Zolberg, Suhrke, and Aguayo 1989) The Tamil diasporic community's numbers are upward of eight hundred thousand (De-Votta 2009). It is now known that voluntarily and through the intimidation, authoritarianism, and shrewd international organizing of the LTTE, the Tamil diaspora played a significant role in sustaining the conflict. Ideologically, they did so through the rhetoric of separatism globally and through their financial contributions. Scholars have argued that the diaspora sustained the war. According to Sarah Wayland, "remittances to Sri Lanka have surpassed US$1 billion since 1999" and "account for 5 percent of Sri Lanka's gross national product" (2004, 422). The Tigers played on the fragility of the refugee community, many of whom were working class, held guilt for leaving the country, and had strong familial connections left behind. This dominance of the LTTE across diasporic communities was to the loss of the Tamil population inside that was under the control of the LTTE and used as a recruiting ground for its war.

I am a dancer of Sri Lankan Tamil descent, produced in diaspora through a different circumstance—that of British Empire. My family members based in Malaysia were very much aware of the war in Sri Lanka. Many still had ties, along with a deep nostalgia for the embattled city of the north and their homeland, Jaffna. As a Malaysian born–Sri Lankan, I was separate from a diaspora produced through war, yet my family's migration to Canada intersected with the waves of Tamil refugees to the country, and I circulated with Tamil friends who escaped the war. In Sri Lanka my "not-from-here" status was read on my body and in my papers. My U.S. passport made me less suspect, as I appeared removed from the large Tamil diaspora in Toronto, Canada. Yet like most, during the period of escalation leading up to final stage of the war, travel across the country was restricted to official business.

Not only is war central to this book, but it is the frame in which this project exists. My initial desire was to consider bharata natyam across regions and the diverse communities in Sri Lanka. This was not possible with the dissolution of the Cease-Fire Agreement and the escalation of war. Thus, the project itself centers on Colombo and bharata natyam practitioners with whom I found myself speaking, learning, and dancing.

Dance and Ethnicity in Sri Lanka

The prolonged civil war shaped both dance and dancers who attempted to maintain normalcy. Choreography permits a sense of choice in a space and time where there can be little to no choosing. Thus, selections of movement along with the dancers' experiences maneuvering the streets of the safe-but-not-so-safe city of Colombo weighed on each other, shifting meanings of movement and the body both onstage and in streets. Assigned to occupy and hold space as markers of identities significant both historically as actors in what some conceive to be a long-standing primordial conflict and as contemporary actors in the twentieth-century civil war, bodies and dance tousled for symbolic and material space. In a nation where all are affected by war, bodies and movement carry a meaning burdened with representation beyond the dancers—not of their own choosing—alluding to ancient warring actors or contemporary ones. Both dance and body are implicated and appropriated into the battle. At the same time dance embodies and embeds these dimensions of war.

As I discuss in chapter 1, the emergence of bharata natyam dance on concert stages and within organizations prior to the country's independence from Britain in 1948 showcased a more inclusive concept of Sri Lanka and Sri Lankans, not parceled in terms of ethnicity. But the "recontextualization" of the Buddhist ritual practice *kohomba kankariya* into Kandyan dance or the national dance of Sri Lanka in 1956 during a period of rising Sinhala nationalism aided the bleeding of nation-state politics into embodied movement (Reed 2010). The intertwining of dance and ethnic identity—Tamil to bharata natyam; Sinhala to Kandyan—referenced as obvious in the performed choreography of *Gaja Vadana/Gajaga Vannam* described at the opening of this text, would be woven during the 1950s rise of postcolonial nationalism that would lead up to the conflict. As I discuss in chapter 2 and the conclusion, emerging cultural nationalism utilized "difference" as a means of development through state-led projects but also through neoliberal types of assistance (e.g., international aid) that assigned specific types of labor and arts practice as worthy and uplifting of society.

Moving Bodies, Navigating Conflict tells of the ways in which practitioners, predominantly women, sustain dance practice in the unstable political and geographic landscape of war. Placing women at the center of my analysis, I discuss how dancers choreograph, teach, perform, and produce. Existing in this hybrid island, dance can address and define ethnic identity in ways that reject the hybridity that informs the practice. Yet dance is also given a desired symbolic value that hides undesired bodies, while dancing can be a means of inserting bodies to ascribe them value.

In this text I speak of what Judith Butler calls a "performative contradiction," where the symbolic value of practice rubs against the bodies practicing, inviting further exploration of its place and its work (Butler and Spivak 2007, 63–66). If, as Butler suggests, "there can be no radical politics of change without performative contradiction," then this study embraces the contradictions to locate the radical politics within it (66). Dance and dancing is a gendered practice, and the role of women as implementing and asserting cultural value through their bodies and their movements calls for an investigation of their navigations as women, dancers, teachers, choreographers, and producers that imagine and deploy their own representations during war. I discuss their subversive strategies to make visible discussions of identity and experiences silenced and omitted by structures of surveillance, militarization, nationalism, and even dance. The practice of bharata natyam possesses many labels — Tamil, global, Indian, and Sri Lankan, and each carry political significance.

Paying attention to the gendered experience of war is necessary. Neloufer De Mel points out that with the rise of the security regime because of the war, "there is a vivid interplay of security and gender: of masculinized militarism and gendered insecurity that have their corollary in violence against women and the marginalisation of women's labor" (2009, 36) Many productions discussed here are organized by senior women who are the last of family to reside in Sri Lanka; their children, siblings and relatives emigrated to escape the conflict. Selvy Thiruchandran (1999) reminds us that the material reality of war is the disturbance of the normative. Her study of the war in eastern Sri Lanka has shown an increase of female heads of home, which have created leadership patterns different from patriarchal patterns of domination. The women artists that inform this study are privileged enough to afford dance — they are from the lower-middle to upper-middle classes. Living in Colombo, these artists experienced a different type of patrol than those in the east or north. As artists, they enjoy an amount of freedom and trust — a rare experience — especially over those who sought refuge from areas of war and are new to the city.

Often, with conflict and dance, audiences are interested in a specific form of the politicization of movement. In the case of Sri Lanka, many are interested in how the form was used in support of the separatist struggle through the Tigers' investment in cultural production. Such works are highlighted in Janet O'Shea's chapter, "From Temple to Battlefield," in the anthology *Choreographies of 21st Century Wars*. O'Shea considers this representation as part of a "revolutionary strategy" through its support of the separatist movement. She also offers two other examples of bharata natyam to be read as intersecting with war yet differing in representation and what is done with dance: a neutrality that is apolitical and a practice that affords reconciliation between groups made opposed through nationalism (2016, 114). *Moving Bodies, Navigating Conflict* does not limit politicization to particular expressions of art tied to the separatist struggle or electoral politics. It does explore many modes of dance practice that may often be read as neutral from the recognized politics of war. I am invested in reading how politics shapes what is performed and what is received as neutral yet is politically constructed. These analytic navigations by the choreographer, student, performer, or even researcher may take place in the studio, behind or on the stage, or after the performance. I remind myself that a critical transnational feminist study does not aim to predict (feminist) politics or find a singular transnational form of feminist work but is open to its multivalence and variance (Swarr and Nagar 2010). This book considers power in movement, in its multiple forms.

Technique and Vocabulary (Methodology)

I locate individual, performed enactments within larger geographies of power. As this text moves between stage, studio, and street, I expose the self-making that takes place in the embodied practice of dance alongside the nation making produced by the everyday patterns of war. This analysis sees how each speaks to the other and how disparities within each mode (of dance and of war) are expressed. Consolidating varied foci of dance theory and dance studies with ethnography, *Moving Bodies, Navigating Conflict* pays attention to the meaning of movement in its varied forms of engagement and aims to be cognizant of its multilayered local and global significance. Influenced by the analytic insights of Marta Savigliano's (1995) ethnography on the tango, which articulates a "political economy of passion," and Anna Scott's (1997) work on *bloco afro* and its commodification under "world dance," this book considers issues of ethnic identity, its appropriation, and its circulation through dance. Feminist in their methods, Savigliano's and Scott's ethnographic works border on autobiography in their reflexivity to consider what aspects of "self" are important filters through which information flows. And as Gay Morris and Jens Giersdorf state in their introduction to *Choreographies of 21st Century Wars*, "Viewing war through the concept of choreography is significant because it shifts the focus of study away from the abstractions of political and military theory to corporeal agency" (2016, 2). Embodiment is the vehicle for understanding throughout this text and permits me not only to consider agency but to understand *movement*, the performance, under disciplinary frameworks of nation, war, and even dance.

Engaging in feminist ethnography, I address the ways in which my body is already implicated in the "field" site. As a diasporic practitioner, I too am interested in the ways in which my own body informs my understanding of the dance and its practice. My body visibly "fits" in the politics and ethnic labels of Sri Lanka, even though I am a third-generation Sri Lankan Tamil from Malaysia presently living in Canada. Similarly, familial experiences—paternal aunties who studied the form in Malaysia and cousins who earned their diplomas in dance in India—frame my approach and learning of the dance form. My training in the dance form is diasporic; I studied the form in both Canada and the United States. This type of experience and familiarity with the dance practice also influences the reading and "acceptance" of my body in the field. The kinesthetic response I felt living in Colombo, subjected to security checks like a local citizen and frequently questioned about my last name, my origins, and my reasons for being in the country, brought home the ways in which I fit within a complex system of identity and knowledge.

My body not only was received and read in the field but was actively being created in it. My circulations among specific communities shaped my viewpoints of being a Tamil woman from the diaspora, and it shaped my perceptions of the conflict. With dancing and in my own travels, my body was being disciplined to understand what's right and what's wrong, to attempt to fit in through a sense of accomplishment in communication, exchange, and reception. My dance practice often became a measure from which others deviated or aligned. The dancers with whom I dance and studied with and I exchanged viewpoints made in our homes and in our practices. What was being made? What is unmade? How did I change?

I am invested in bringing the mundane (the repetition of steps, the going and coming from rehearsals) and the spectacle (the breadth of staged performance, the clear instances of violence) in a focused study of dance in one locale: Colombo, Sri Lanka. Identity is inscribed geographically. Identity marks bodies, and bodies mark areas, blocks, and neighborhoods in

Colombo. Yet dancers negotiate space not only physically onstage but spatially within the ideological formation of the nation. What space is afforded them? Many Tamil families have left Colombo in the decades since the start of the war, after state-supported pogroms mass-murdered Tamils in the city in 1983 or as the government forcibly bussed Tamils out of the city during my time in the field in 2007, making them to return to their "homes," literally in battlefields. Dance schools throughout the city that at one time prospered were by 2007 barely occupied. These migrations have changed the cultural geography and makeup of the city and the neighborhoods within it, declaring areas "safe" for some and "unsafe" for others. Tracking bharata natyam dance through the space and time of this urban landscape exposes the prolonged conflict and the immediate experiences of fear that shaped dance practice and its meaning in a local setting.

Yet *Moving Bodies, Navigating Conflict* is also a teasing out of how the body and dance are interpellated within global circulations of culture, economics, and bodies. To discuss the global significance of the local Sri Lankan dancer may seem a far stretch. Sri Lanka was of little importance in global news circuits unless scenes of newsworthy violence were taking place. But the Tigers and the government of Sri Lanka were well aware of their positioning among global powers, using such knowledge to revamp their nationalism and legitimize brute force, whether in their discussions of sovereignty and free will or when grappling with large diasporic populations of Tamil and Sinhala exiles and emigrants who left the island. Like so many postcolonial nations that celebrated independence with a lack—the debt to be paid in positioning oneself within a larger colonial-dominate global market—Sri Lanka became the recipient of "giving" through aid and development projects that also employ the arts. In terms of popular global form, the juggernaut of Indian cinema, Kollywood and Bollywood and its popular dance styles, cannot be dismissed or disassociated from discussions of local circulations of bharata natyam and Kandyan dance in Sri Lanka. Like the war, dance in Sri Lanka not only resonates with local significance but also is inflected by larger scales of the global.

From an outside perspective, bharata natyam dance may be viewed simply as an Indian dance form that migrated to the island nation. It is in part a reconstructed, "revived" Indian national dance produced from the temple dance tradition of the *devadasis*, the matriarchal community of temple performing artists. The works of Amit Srinivasan (1985) and Avanthi Meduri (1996) locate the female dancing body in economic and cultural transformations taking place toward the later years of the British Raj, rising Indian nationalism, and the emergence of the postcolonial Indian state. But as dance scholars have probed the significance of bharata natyam outside the era and borders of its "revival" in India, they have noted the flexibility of the form in connoting a meaning and intention of its contemporary practitioners. O'Shea's substantive exploration of bharata natyam as a global form, including among her examples choreographies by artists in the Sri Lankan diaspora in Canada, shows that contemporary meanings assigned to the dance are tied strongly to the form's revival years and its position within colonial, anticolonial, and Indian nationalist movements.[12] O'Shea states, "Individual dancers diverge in their understanding of what the most important aspect of the dance form's history is, how best to express allegiance to that history, and what elements of dance practice should be maintained or revivified" (2007, 28–29).

In Sri Lanka, however, such pick-and-choose approaches must be inserted in a different context—that of war—which amplifies allegiances to land, history, and people. Disparate readings of the island's history form the rationale for the contemporary conflict, entwining religious and linguistic arguments with historical ones (Tenekoon 1990). The dancer engages directly with this rationale, entwining similarly religious references and language choices along with their own experience to produce a (counter) cultural response, creating their own measure and rationale of the politics of nation, dance, their own bodies, and the war.

Bharata natyam practice intersects with regionally specific politics on multiple levels, to reveal discords between state led understandings of bharata natyam as "Indian" or "foreign" and meanings attributed to the form by local dance practitioners as "indigenous" and "Tamil." Bharata natyam practice and its implementation on local and national stages demonstrates an ethnically marked contentiousness, exposing its belonging to or rejection from the Sri Lanka nation-state. Sri Lanka is unique in that dance is integral to the state, both in terms of histories of nationalism, as I discuss in chapter 1, and in terms of contemporary state education, as I discuss in chapter 2. State-sponsored recontextualization of Buddhist practice into the concert form of Kandyan dance was created in partial response to the growing popularity of bharata natyam among young women and girls across boundaries of ethnicity and religion (but not class or caste) in Sri Lanka and across the South Asian diaspora. Susan Reed's insightful and in-depth research historicizes the transformation or "recontextualization," as she puts it, of the Buddhist theater ritual, kohomba kankariya, a male-only dance and drumming practice, into Kandyan dance, the national dance of Sri Lanka, during the Sinhala nationalist revival of 1956. Reed shows that the dance, initially labeled "Sinhala dance," was by 1956 labeled "national" or "Kandyan," essentially masking its ethnic exclusiveness.

Kandyan dance would incorporate bharata natyam's "feminine" movement qualities to make it a form attractive to young Sinhala women (Reed 2010, 203). The labeling of Kandyan dance and its associated national significance revealed through Reed's historical and anthropological study is integral to understanding the circulating significance and meaning attributed to bharata natyam practice in Colombo. It highlights how one ethnic dance was transformed to become representative of the entire nation during a period of Sinhala ethnic nationalism. Demonstrating how dance practice is ethnically marked in Sri Lanka, Reed's analysis shows how Kandyan dance was created in response to a dance practice deemed not Sri Lankan—bharata natyam, a practice that appealed to Colombo's ethnically diverse population.

With the *Gaja Vadana/Gajaga Vannam*, the bharata natyam dance that incorporated Kandyan dance movements, which opened the discussion, this book examines how choreographic choices mask several strategies ripe for closer queries: Is the *Gaja Vadana/Gajaga Vannam* a performed acknowledgment of identity and difference through the juxtaposition of dance forms? Does it illuminate a need for the Tamil choreographer to actively engage with a Sinhala form, Kandyan dance, as a friendly gesture for inclusion or for political and financial gain within a larger dance economy? Is it, to borrow again from Butler, a "performative contradiction" (Butler and Spivak 2007)? Choreographies in dance mark resistance and negotiation with local and larger circulations of dance culture. It is necessary, then, to read movement among its many forms, whether bharata natyam, Kandyan, or Western contemporary, alongside the politics of Sri Lanka and its conflict. As Homi Bhabha states, "The transnational dimension of cultural transformation—migration, diaspora, displacement, relocations—turns the specifying or localizing process of cultural translation into a complex process of signification" (1992, 49).

Ethnography, as an everyday practice, pays attention to the ordinary attached to a prolonged war: it exposes the ways in which dance is an everyday mode through which identity, nationalism, contested histories, and progressive visions are produced and staged. Providing a "sociology of culture," to use Raymond Williams's (1995) terms, daily negotiations of the state and the body are understood through embodied analysis, whether processes of dance pedagogy, choreography, production, or performance. Bodies and their experiences are typically left out of discussions of conflict that focus on politics and policy. Both are interconnected here, and this text aims to make transparent the process of producing subjectivity through the acquiring and performing of disciplined movement. Engagement with dance and war demands attention beyond staged presentation, with an equal willingness to examine the everyday. For, to borrow Julie Taylor's interpretation of the words of Doris Salcedo, Colombian sculptor and visual artist, "In the media they are showing you the particularities of the dead, they are not showing you the dimensions of death," I would similarly affirm: on the stage they are showing you the particularities of form, not the dimensions of the practice itself (1998, 60). I use dance ethnography to attend to "indirect revelations of terror" through dance: its hint-laced exchanges and nuanced aesthetics that mark a constant awareness of potential violence and everyday war (61).

Choreography (Chapters)

Throughout I explore a range of choreographies, locales, and texts; I show how multiple and varied spaces and ways of entering and practicing construct, reinscribe, and put into question the dance's association with identity, state, and the transnational. In the first half of the book, chapters 1 and 2, I consider at length the implications of hybridity and dance in the emerging postcolonial nation and the nation at war. I examine institutional frames of the dance that emerged during the years leading to and following Ceylon's independence from Britain by looking at the roles of social reform movements, community organizations, and state education. In the second half of the book—chapters 3 and 4—I consider choreographies and the processes of production, examining choices made in productions, in studios, and in the in-between, on the streets of Colombo. The framing of ethnicity and arguments of difference projected onto the dance by institutions and the theoretical discourses espoused by them are critiqued through the moving bodies—the practitioners—who reveal disruptions between practice and theory, between dance and identity. Unifying both parts of the text is the consideration of embodiment embracing both the moving body and experiences of subjectivity.

Within these two sections the following chapters foreground my concerns with understanding how the practice of dance is shaped by conflict. Situating subjectivity in the midst of postcolonial politics and emerging conflict, chapter 1 analyzes local *herstories* of bharata natyam practice in Colombo to demonstrate that as identity and difference became central in the years leading up to and after Ceylon's independence from Britain, so did it become embodied and performed through the dance. Speaking to practitioners, I show that these dancing bodies, becoming more patrolled on the stage and the streets of Colombo with the rise of nationalism and war, maintained a keen awareness of the politics surrounding the form, their bodies, and the changing landscape around them. Made visible through the dancers' recollections is the production of nationalism through dancing bodies and the maneuvering of choreography on stages that were becoming more and more politicized. In paying attention to the dancing practitioner, I show how women's dancing bodies were spoken of, but women's experiences with the dance practice are unacknowledged.

Pushed into a politics of difference whose grasp grew stronger with the postcolonial nation-state, dance and the dancer became ethnicized on an exclusively Sri Lankan stage. Examining the localized practice and localized politics of dance in Sri Lanka allows for an understanding of how the practice is made distinct from an Indian-centered discourse or source. Kalakshetra bharata natyam, a specific style of bharata natyam from South India and a practice that embraced individuals across religious and ethnic boundaries in Colombo, would later emerge as a marker of Tamil identity for many Tamils. The significance ascribed to bharata natyam dance and Kalakshetra bharata natyam demonstrated a growing need to assert a Tamil historicity, belonging, and visible presence in Sri Lanka. This need would become central to the practice of the dance during the war.

The alignment of dance and identity was assisted by the nation-state and reflected the emerging condition of civil conflict. By 1972 the learning of dance, Kandyan, and bharata natyam became a means to fulfill the "aesthetic requirement," a mandatory subject in all government or public schools. In chapter 2 I discuss how emerging cultural nationalism utilized "difference" as a means of development through neoliberal projects. Exploring the day-to-day work and experiences of bharata natyam teachers alongside the educational policies that introduced the mandated subject, I demonstrate clear unevenness in the distribution and teaching of Kandyan and bharata natyam dance among Sinhala-medium and Tamil-medium schools. I argue that the nation-state, through this requirement of the aesthetics subject, reaffirms Kandyan dance as a Sinhala-only practice, yet separates bharata natyam from the Sri Lankan Tamil body. Through its curricula and uneven distribution, the state clears the way for bharata natyam to be invested in by Sinhala dancing bodies. Yet, I show, in Tamil-medium schools, the practice of offering solely bharata natyam dance to Tamil students to fulfill the requirement simultaneously reaffirms bharata natyam dance as a Tamil practice in Tamil spaces.

Chapter 3 shifts the discussion to analyses of specific choreographies performed in response to the conflict in Sri Lanka in 2007. In their anthology, *Dance, Human Rights, and Social Justice*, Naomi Jackson and Toni Shapiro-Phim discuss the ways in which "dance has been used repeatedly, at different periods in history and in many parts of the world, to promote strict adherence to repressive ideologies," while being "a powerful vehicle for revealing, resisting and rectifying differing forms of abuse and injustices" (2008, xv). Closely reading selected choreographies, I reveal the various strategies of female choreographers who are using dance to address the war in a climate that often silences citizens from discussing the topic in public. I expose discreet negotiations of ethnic identity taking place within these choreographies, informed by circulating meanings ascribed to the dance, the ethnic compositions of the bodies dancing and watching, and the shifting experience of living in the city during an escalating civil war.

Exploring two works about war in Sri Lanka reveals how some Tamil practitioners look to the dance as tradition and imbue the form with vital resistance to Sinhala domination and the state. Additionally, these choreographies demonstrate how bharata natyam dance practice has created spaces to reflect on the ethnic conflict within the context of silence and repression in Sri Lanka. Finally, these pieces reveal how one particular Tamil woman and choreographer navigated geographies of exclusion and ethnic identity in Colombo due to the conflict and strategically choreographed works according to those geographies and the ethnic makeup of these locations. This choreographer not only strategically employed bharata natyam to cater to multiple audiences and groups of dancers but also shaped these choices according to circulating meaning about the form in conjunction with the ever-changing terrain of the city of Colombo as war escalated. Her choreographic navigation of the audiences, dancers, and geographic settings of Colombo illuminate the strategic ways in which citizens—particularly Tamil citizens—themselves maneuvered the civil war in Sri Lanka.

Chapter 4 continues the analysis of choreography through an exploration of process of production, looking at nationally televised dance production. On July 14, 2007, I, along with nine professional Sri Lankan bharata natyam dancers, performed the opening number for the season finale of *Shakthi Superstar*, a Tamil-language, Sri Lankan version of *American Idol*. Beginning with a multiethnic bharata natyam dance company, the piece shifted in terms of both choreography and ensemble to meet the demands of the finale's producers, who wanted a "Bollywood"-style production. Beginning with only trained bharata natyam performers, the piece incorporated—late in the process—a substantial number of Kandyan dancers, all of whom were ethnically Sinhala. These demands and the process they engendered revealed navigations of transnational circulations of culture. What seemingly was an "insignificant" piece of entertainment, the dance became a means for a minority population to make visible their participation in Sri Lankan life and the nation-state.

I conclude with an exploration of dance, postwar. Returning to the country after the unexpected and brutal end to the twenty-six-year civil war, I revisit bharata natyam dance after periods of two and five years. I consider how dance is being used in reconciliation, development, and diplomatic programs for the state, foreign governments, and international nongovernmental organizations. I consider how dance is still contested in postwar Sri Lanka, where violence has gripped campuses over the staging of dance. I return to discuss the utilization of difference in neoliberal development projects in Sri Lanka and tie that to the usage of different "homes" in the growing neoliberal academy in the United States and Canada.

1

Meaning Making

Bharata Natyam as a Transnational Practice in Translation

As we wait for the arrival of the students and teachers at Kalalaya School of Music and Dance, I, along with Daya Mahinda, the school's president, strategically position ourselves in wooden chairs beneath the breeze of the whirling and tenuously swirling ceiling fans. The fans provide us respite from the afternoon heat and sun. My skin is moist with the humidity; the damp sleeves of my *khameez* grip my arms, forcing me to be still. It is only the two of us in the large open space of the school's main hall, where music and dance classes are held. The theater at the front of the hall is empty as well, the drapes shut. The only other faces in the room are those in the framed photographs of the women's organization's founders and former presidents, taken in homes and outdoors in the adjacent yard. Some pose with subtle smiles; others look stoically into the camera. There are plaques with names of members and leaders. There are two black-and-white photos of one clearly notable event: the visit to the school by former Indian president Jawaharlal Nehru and his sister, Vijaya Lakshmi Pandit.

While we sit in the chairs and gaze through the open windows of the auditorium, Mahinda shares a short reflection, one of several in the years to come:

> I think in a way my father took a very strong step by getting us onto the stage because in those days most people thought that if you were from a traditional family, you should not dance—that it would jeopardize one's future. However, our future was fine. I would say that I am like this today because of that wonderful experience of learning dance. Although we were not professionals, we worked very hard to learn dance. And look at me now; I still remember the *jatiswarams* I learned. I remember the *kirtanams* I learned.[1] In those days, unlike today, there were very few dance students. And, as I said, it wasn't the norm for girls of our status to take part in performances onstage, nonetheless dance onstage. We were actually creating a trend.

Portraits of the founders and leaders of the Ceylon Tamil Women's Union at Kalalaya. Photo by the author.

Why was Mahinda not allowed to dance at first and eventually allowed later? What were the implications of dancing and how and why did they shift? As one of three daughters of a prominent, Cinnamon Gardens–based power couple, Mahinda, along with her two sisters, was one of the first Tamil bharata natyam students in Colombo.[2] As I would learn through interviews with senior Tamil bharata natyam practitioners like herself, they were not the first students of bharata natyam in the city. All of them recalled a Sinhala dancer to be the first from Colombo to train in the form extensively. If the earliest practitioner is remembered to be Sinhala, what is hidden by the present reception and larger understanding of the dance? How does the dance become a marker of Tamilness, one accepted as such by the state, demonstrated through images of the form printed on currency, stamps, and billboards? How do we interpret this sign?

Mahinda saw herself as a trendsetter, and I knew that *I* was an outcome of the work and experiences of early practitioners like her. Yet the trajectory of the form, from one suspect to one embraced, from one that is not inherently Tamil to one that is considered as so, was intriguing to me. Janet O'Shea's formidable work on bharata natyam as a global form considers how the revival of the form from 1923 to 1948 would "craft a genealogy in which bharata natyam came to represent ancient tradition and critical experimentation, nationalism, regional identities, and the global transference of forms outside of geographical and cultural boundaries." Overlapping with this period, the form's continuation "depended on this relationship to politics" (2007, 4). This chapter is invested in analyzing the narrative of this cultural sign in its circulation in the city of Colombo. If the form's practice is dependent on politics, as O'Shea proposes, I discuss its local and state-sanctioned relationships. Yet such local and state relationships are not isolated from "global transference" and movements. Local narratives, as discussed here and in subsequent chapters, shape and are shaped by the global, in expansive forms of cultural practice, and in the material, with development and aid.

In "Freedom's Basis in the Indeterminate," Homi Bhabha states, "Culture as a strategy of survival is both transnational and translational." Culture is transnational, he says, because contemporary postcolonial discourses are rooted in histories of displacement, movement, and migration. Culture is translational, he says, because such spatial histories of movement make the question of "how culture signifies or what is signified by culture, rather complex issues" (1992, 47). These two themes, the transnational and the translational, are useful here in this study. The transnational conjures the hybrid island, a port of influence in the Indian Ocean: a terrain so desired it influenced migration, trade, and war. The transnational summons the postcolonial island-state that experienced uneven, yet persistent, European colonialism for 350 years, which designates its means of entrance into the enclosure of "modernity." It speaks to a civil war, marked by nationalism and separatist armed struggle, that merged with an economy of international aid. Bharata natyam is the cultural sign in translation. It is situated cultural knowledge meaningful in embodied and visual forms. Reading the form as transnational and translational allows for a hybridity that undoes a notion of recognition of position or identification "in ways that assumed that we are all fixed and frozen in our various locations and subject positions" (Butler, qtd. in De Alwis 2009, 91).

This chapter considers how bharata natyam in Colombo exposes identity situated and produced through its inseparable placement in the midst of identities beyond itself (Bhabha 1992). That is, taking apart the dance form speaks to the interpellation of an exclusive practice with other bodies, each made distinct through formations—developments, creations, constructions, establishments, realizations, materializations, arrangements, foundations, configurations, choreographies—of caste and class, ethnicity and nationality, and uniquely gendered social mores. The imagined identities that fall outside and within this dancing body—the bharata natyam dancer—are theorized, hailed, and vilified, through myth, stories, and histories *and* confronted in the real through the practice of dance and the experience of war.

The material reality does not always confirm the imagined, but both the real and the imagined continuously shape the dance and the dancers' performance. Can the ethnographer, enmeshed in the rhetoric constructed alongside the practice of the form, alongside the sufferings of war, remove herself from these ideologies, these practices imprinted on her body? These fictions of identity are even absorbed into the body and practice of the ethnographer, who experiences empathy for the narratives and finds herself attached to the trajectory of overcoming grief by the undoing of war.[3] Identities reshape themselves through the dance and writing of dance, and the ethnographer wants to recognize her own form and position in this tale. This chapter traces the narratives of bharata natyam, transnationally, to unpack its association and disassociation with identity and state—to allow for its movement. Embodiment is the means through which this narrative is accessed and understood.

Debates of Identity in the Early Twentieth Century

"It wasn't the norm for girls of our status to take part in performances onstage, nonetheless dance onstage," Mahinda states. As high-class and high-caste Vellalar Tamil girls, Mahinda and her two other sisters were raised in a conservative family. This meant that outside of preliminary and secondary schooling, they were expected to spend most of their time inside the home. Activities, like dance, were not "the norm" for girls of her status. In the nineteenth century the movement of Arumuka Navalar (1822–79), the Jaffna-born, Vellalar, Tamil, and Hindu social reformer, greatly inspired and propagated dance and dancers' ill repute. He, as well as many other Hindu and Tamil elites, vilified temple dancers as sources of disease and social problems. *Sadir*, the dance practice of the devadasis, had "connotations of an unrefined play with sexual meanings." Ethical texts released during the period advised young children not to even "look" at dance because it was considered sinful (Thiruchandran 1998, 38).

Disclosing this history to scholars of the region and the dance while in the United States, I was instructed to consider the devadasi dance practice in Colombo. According to dance historian Davesh Soneji, "long before the anti-nautch debates begin in South India, dance by devadasis in temples was publically condemned in Sri Lanka in the context of a larger Saiva religious reform movement spearheaded by Arumuka Navalar" (2010, 41). In "Śiva's Courtesans" Soneji establishes that these dancers utilized rhetorical strategies of the institutions that disparaged them—whether social reformers or nationalists—and defended their practices through weaving the historical and spiritual lineages of their bodies and their dance. He discusses one particular Colombo-based devadasi, Ancukam, who authored the text *Uruttira-kanikaiyar* in 1911. According to Soneji (2010), the structure of *Uruttirakani-kaiyar* establishes Ancukam's lineage as connected to the courtesans of the Hindu god Shiva, from Puranic texts of the third to tenth century CE. Soneji argues that the rhetorical strategies of *Uruttirakanikaiyar* demonstrate a recognition of the animosity toward and mistrust of dancing women and deploys a counterstrategy to trace histories of self, profession, and the dance practice as long-standing and embedded in spiritual or religious ritual to "open up the space of nation and citizenship" for devadasis (2010, 32).

Mahinda didn't speak of Navalar or devadasis but made clear a notion of "status" based on caste and class. Her story was familiar to me. My own appreciation of learning dance was driven through its absence in my mother's life. As a child, I was often told stories of how she, my mother, was barred from learning dance by my grandmother and found herself peeking through the windows of the dance school, watching the dancers move in class. Mahinda didn't frame the initial refusal of dance on social reform or notions of temple dances; status was located in the framework of caste and cultural discrimination. This sense of caste and cultural difference was expressed, in large part, through gendered practices.

The Vellalar are a land-owning caste whose dominance educationally and monetarily in the northern peninsula would also secure Jaffna as the center of Elam, the Tamil homeland, for part of the civil war.[4] Vellalar status was hinged on women and the so-called chastity tied to social relations and work (or leisure). Its discriminatory world was also one that created an Other through a sense of civilization, domesticity, and labor. Such discrimination was not only isolated to the Wanniya Laeto, who are misnamed the Vedda, a term that translates to "jungle" or "forest," to convey them as "uncivilized" people who fall outside of distinguished caste. In his studies of Tamil culture in Sri Lanka, Bryan Pfaffenberger states,

> The association of un-chastity and lowered status is clearly shown
> in the beliefs about the Veddahs, and indeed Vellalars liken the so-
> called Minority Tamils, the two Untouchable laboring castes (Nalavar

and Pallar), to jungle folk. The association is driven home in everyday economic activity, for Vellalars prefer to hire Untouchable women in their rice fields and for gathering fodder, thus ensuring the common Jaffna vista of unchaperoned Untouchable women walking about in public. The chastity value is disputed by no one, but it nonetheless is a value tinged with the reality of Vellalar domination. (1981, 1150)

Pfaffenberger's observations take place in a time leading up to the war. Today the Jaffna Peninsula continues to experience varied stratifications of caste and class, but I can only *imagine* that the vista, after twenty-six years of war, has changed, as the peninsula was one of many sites of contests with the state and now, postwar, of ongoing surveillance and development by the state.

Nonetheless, Pfaffenberger's work exposes the ways in which caste projects itself on to women and their social norms—reflected in Mahinda's words, "girls of our status" barred from dance practice.[5] Selvy Thiruchandran discusses how the female body was at the center of Tamil revival and social reform (the movement headed by Navalar) and cites an editorial published in the *Hindu Organ*, a Jaffna-based paper, where five components of an ideal education for Tamil women were listed. The list demonstrates caste, classed, and religious chauvinism through gendered practice. The five components were listed: Hindu religion, so Tamil women would not be converted; Tamil literature, but not Western literature or the Western system of education; hygiene, to know how to cook nutritious food and how to nurse and care for the sick; music (but specifically not dance), so they can please their husband and others in the home; and physical exercise, to bear healthy children (1998, 89). Tamil daughters were raised to demonstrate the four qualities of an acceptable Tamil woman: fear (of doing the wrong thing), innocence, shyness, and chastity (91). These qualities were believed to shape the ideal Tamil wife and mother. They were, then, to be expressed in every aspect of the contemporary Tamil women's behavior: body language, dress, sex segregation, confinement of young girls from public life, only home schooling for girls (Schrijvers 1999, 178; Thiruchandran 1998, 83–92). The maintenance of a Tamil girl's "honor" through these practices was essential to the status of her family and caste (Pfaffenberger 1981). The ideal Tamil woman was an ideal wife and mother, and dance did not fit within those criteria.

The social reform was an anticolonial strategy. Yet it was influenced by, not only responsive to, the West. As Ancukam was responding to the rhetoric of Navalar, Navalar himself was informed by rhetorical strategies he learned through the Methodist missionary school he attended in Jaffna. Navalar assisted in the translation of the Bible to Tamil, made many innovations in writing, and introduced public speaking in Tamil (Kailasapathy 1979, 33). The "concerted missionary effort" in Jaffna, "which in the nineteenth century threatened to overwhelm the Hindu religion with a tide of Christian conversions," led to a reform movement that espoused the classed and caste values of the Jaffna Peninsula (Pfaffenberger 1981, 1150).

Overlapping with the Tamil social reform movement, which was couched within Hindu practice as espoused by Navalar, was a Buddhist revival, which assisted in the development of an exclusively Sinhala Ceylonese nationalism. A central figure of the movement was Angarika Dharmapala (1864–1933), a Buddhist Theosophist. According to Tessa Bartholomeusz, "Dharmapala argued that Ceylon Buddhism needed to reformed, and that it should be reformed in accordance with the ancient texts." He also wanted to purge the religion of any "superstition" (1994, 44). As a Theosophist, Dharmapala promoted canonical Buddhism as an ideal for Buddhist society, and through his focus on ancient texts he determined that women could play a great part in the making of an ideal Buddhist world. Similarly gendered as the reforms of Navalar, as Dharmapala considered women as sources of temptation that would lead to the ruin of male renunciants, laywomen could also take on religious knowledge and practice. This would lead Dharmapala to promoting the "canonical" practice of female renunciation.

The Buddhist revival spearheaded by Dharmapala and the Hindu social reform movement led by Navalar were oppositional to the colonial project yet incorporated what Stephen Prothero terms "nineteenth-century academic Orientalism," elevating the importance of text over local ritual and religious practice (1995, 294). This was assisted strongly by the American Theosophical movement, whose founder and president Col. Henry Steel Olcott (1832–1907) had settled the international organization in Adyar, near what is now Chennai, and assisted Dharmapala in founding the worldwide Buddhist organization, the Maha Bodhi Society, in 1891 in what was then Ceylon. Prothero states that Olcott "viewed modern Hinduism and Buddhism as 'but brutalizations of their primal types.'" He would engage in teaching what practicing Hindus and Buddhists should do:

> In addition to legitimizing his reform agenda, Olcott's split of Asian religious traditions into their laudable ancient and lamentable modern

manifestation fueled his racialism. If he avoided the missionaries' tendency to decry Asians as heathen, he shared the Orientalists' penchant for viewing them as a lesser breed. (295)

Ancient sutras were "perfect," yet contemporary Hindus and Buddhists were abominations of their own classical heritage. But through texts and attention to daily observances as proscribed in such lists published in the *Hindu Organ*, the laity would be able to observe their religions in proper form. It is not that didactic texts did not exist in Tamil literature but that the social reform movements incorporated external influences into local religious practices.

The practices condoned by social reformers were transnational and translational, incorporating the ideologies of Western Orientalists in anti-Western practices. Antagonistic identities were rubbing against one another. In Orientalism the "Oriental" was the object of the past or a diminutive present as translated through this transnational interaction (Said 1978). The "Oriental" could self-actualize as a conditional subject through social reform composed of practice deemed respectable, proper, and demonstrative of modernity by external forces. But these practices were not only to be tied to individuals. In taking on a protestant approach, collective social reform was essential (Prothero 1995, 292).

Laywomen would be important to the making of collective social reform, in both Buddhist and Hindu social reform movements. According to Bartholomeusz, during the 1890s women participated in activities to revive Buddhism as lay preachers of the religion and "to the dismay of many" began wearing ocher-colored robes like those worn by the *sangha*, or the Buddhist monastic community (1994, 10). The two elite Tamil women's organizations that would become mainstays in discussing the history of bharata natyam practice in the city took on this commitment to collective social reform. Incorporating the ideas from the social reform movements, these organizations were established in Colombo to counter the effects of colonialism and what they identified as cultural miscegenation. They would emerge as the primary sites for the learning of bharata natyam dance in Colombo. The Ceylon Tamil Women's Union was founded in 1909 ("Kalalayathin" 1998). Saiva Mangaiyar Kalagam was formed in 1930 ("Saiva Mangaiyar Vidyalayam" 1998, 24). Although Saiva Mangaiyar Kalagam was a Hindu Tamil organization, and the Ceylon Tamil Women's Union was founded by both Christian and Hindu Tamil women, both organizations viewed Tamil culture as threatened by the miscegenation with British culture through colonialism.

With nostalgic sentiments the missions of these organizations reflected a desire to inculcate young women with culture believed to exist prior to the arrival of colonialism. They took on the responsibility to educate young people in specific traditions. The Ceylon Tamil Women's Union "gathered as a cultural organization interested in preserving Tamil culture (dance, theatre and music) in the era of British colonialism and Western influence," whose "spreading of foreign cultures, habits and education" was affecting Tamil ways of life. ("Kalalayathin" 1998). Inaugurated in 1930, Saiva Mangaiyar Kalagam's mission and purpose illuminate the drive to expose young people to Hinduism and Tamil language. An ex-president of the organization reminisced about the organization's founding:

> At a time when our Island was under colonial rule and the younger generation was under the influence of western thought and culture, forgetting their traditional Hindu values, the founding members of the Kalagam reawakened the Hindus, *particularly the women*, from their slumber. It united their resolve to preserve an ancient way of life and to promote the Hindu Dharma through their mother tongue, Tamil. ("President Reminisces" 2000, 20; emphasis added)

In their quests to unearth and remember "tradition" and "culture," both organizations became communalist in the ways in which they attempted to revive a particular Tamil identity that encompassed a whole culture with little differentiation or an acknowledgment of class and caste. Nationalist and communalist discourses in colonial and postcolonial South Asia, like those represented in the letter in the *Hindu Organ*, questioned what of the West was to be permitted to enter cultural and social folds (Thiruchandran 1998; P. Chatterjee, 1990, 238). Both organizations thought of laywomen as being active agents in remembering tradition and maintaining ethnicity and culture. This labor was bound to gender and class as the women of these communities were of the leisure classes; they were not required to participate in a wage-labor economy.

Miscegenation and transnational influence were denied, even though the discourse of social reform as deployed by these Tamil and women's organizations and the practice and lives of devadasis such as Ancukam stretched beyond borders and were shaped by the colonial project. The text of Ancukam endeavored to establish a spiritual lineage that connected her own body and practice to an ancient and spiritual realm. But, as Soneji argues, the desire of Ancukam to claim a religious history failed to acknowledge the courtly setting and influence on the dance: "It is significant that these devadasis were not performing ritual dances. Their tasks, like those of Ancukam and her mother, involved performing court-style dances in the *mandapas* of these temples, a tradition that persisted until the 1960s" (2010, 40). The desire to insert oneself into the ritual tradition was in response to the adversary perceptions of the court traditions and of dancers in general. Such desires and approaches articulated neatly with projects of divorcing the political ("courtly" in earlier historical settings) from a "pure" realm of the religious, where ritual existed and history could be imagined in an unbroken manner. The duties to maintain honor through the practices demanded and expected of women reappears in the narrative of identity and dance in Colombo. Ancukam would view her body as maintaining the past. The women of Saiva Mangaiyar Kalagam and the Tamil Women's Union would also see themselves as actively participating in maintaining (not so much creating) the connection between the past and present through their organizational work in the arts and literature. The written works produced by Saiva Mangaiyar Kalagam and the Tamil Women's Union focused particularly on Tamil women, but they were elite Tamil women. Although these organizations desired a Ceylon free from colonial rule, their writings focused on Tamilness and never discussed the diversity of Sri Lanka.

But, in the words of Mahinda, the current president of the Tamil Women's Union, a sense of ethnic plurality in the dance form emerges through her remembrance of the first dancer of bharata natyam, a young Sinhala girl at the time. She affirms the breaking of tradition in the creation of new ones: "It wasn't the norm for girls of our status to take part in performances onstage, nonetheless dance onstage." Mahinda focuses on the ways in which a new practice is created on specific bodies. In this rhetorical stance she establishes herself as influential to the current-day practice.

Mahinda's access to the dance offered a chance of accomplishment in her later years, as she remembers her body's practice of repertoire. In this acknowledgment there is a sense of laboring and risk. Unlike Ancukam's body, which was presented to maintain a lineage from the divine to the earthly, from antiquity to her time, to justify her own belonging and value, Mahinda can remember her body for the change it made in practice, for being influential. Her words demonstrate that it is those well-situated who are conditionally permitted, within the values of social reform, to "create a trend." We see how participation in dance had the potential to ruin her reputation as well as Ancukam's and jeopardize both their futures, as conceptions of proper Tamil womanhood demanded dance's exclusion. Yet their navigations are different, marked by their dissimilar status and associated sense of agency and belonging. I am left wanting to uncover how, then, did dance become an accepted practice? And where was that first dancer of bharata natyam in Colombo?

Kalakshetra and Discourses of Identity

I am a graduate of Kalakshetra and still associate with it. If I change my dance style, then I cannot face my teachers. We take an oath to stick to Athey's tradition, and I am strictly following that. The new students coming from Sri Lanka, they have totally changed the art form and have ruined the art. They are not fit to use the name "Kalakshetra" because they have ruined its name. In Kalakshetra we do not lift the legs; we do not expose the body, and there are no movements below the hips.

—Rangana, a graduate of Kalakshetra and a bharata natyam teacher in Colombo

Rangana is a Colombo-based senior bharata natyam teacher who received her diploma from Kalakshetra, a dance and arts school in Besant Nagar, near Chennai, India, after completing the five-year course. Her mother, Padma, is the dancer remembered by several senior teachers as the first student from Colombo to learn bharata natyam by going to India. Padma was evoked often in conversations as the first student of bharata natyam and for being Buddhist and Sinhala. The earlier statement was in response to my question: what are your thoughts on experimenting with the form? The discipline of which Rangana speaks veils concepts of respectability situated in caste and class differences that cross what are now-expected boundaries of ethnicity. Her journey to study the form speaks to transnational crossings that have been the marker of not only bharata natyam but Sri Lanka. As required by her pledge or "oath," she resists change to the dance. She doesn't speak of ethnic difference, nor do I ask her too many questions about the matter.

O'Shea (2007) proposes "intersecting dialogues" and "dialogical tensions" through which performers of bharata natyam "configure" the form. One such intersection or tension is tradition and individuality. In her 2002 work, "The Changing Role of Women in Sri Lankan Society," Malathi De Alwis examines Ceylonese womanhood in the colonial and anticolonial eras and states, "Notions of 'tradition' and 'modernity,' 'statis' and 'change' were thus not only intimately intertwined with conceptions of Tamil and Sinhala 'womanhood' but co-constitutive of each other" (2002, 675). Rangana's statement exemplifies the tensions held in the form, how a dancer is cultivated by situating self and art along a seemingly dichotomous pole of tradition and experimentation. Her assertion of allegiance to an artistic discipline differentiates herself and those similarly disciplined from others. She distances herself from others that do not *move* this way.

Rangana's words do not speak of ethnicity, only nationality, and her criticisms are distributed across ethnicity. The question—how does one dance without moving below the hips?—may be an appropriate follow-up to her statement, and the absences in my own query offer a further reading into codes of respectability that continue to frame dancers and selves beyond the studio. It may reveal, so early into this book, a limitation of my own ethnographic inquiry, speaking to the ways in which conflicts onstage alongside those taking place in the streets of Colombo restrain social exchanges. In Bhabha's (1992) notion of culture as transnational and translational, bharata natyam's story in Colombo, Sri Lanka, exposes traversals and transformation along poles of value-laden aesthetics that are situated in Sri Lankan history and contemporary politics and are encountered through bodies and their interactions. Bodies become boundaries (Yuval-Davis and Stoetzler 2002, 329).

Rangana's response to my questions recalls a discipline of the body that ties physical quality of movement and dress to her guru (or teacher), her school, and both of their values. Kalakshetra's approach to movement and women's bodies and the philosophy of bharata natyam as championed by its founder, Rukmini Devi Arundale, fit within gendered practices of the upper classes and castes. The dance amalgamated local knowledges with colonial practices.[6] *Revival* is a term often used in postcolonial performance—and often in discourse on bharata natyam—to describe the process of the creation of bharata natyam dance from the years 1923 to 1948 (O'Shea 2007, 4). Embedded in the term are multiple processes: repopulation (where one community takes a practice from another), reconstruction (changing or rejecting aspects of repertoire); renaming and resituating (the place of practice), and restoration (where the performative invents a new practice and simultaneously a new "historical" one) (Allen 1997, 63–64). Devi, who was respectably referred to as Athey (mother-in-law) or Amma (mother) by her students, is a major actor in the revival of the form in the early twentieth century (Meduri 1996, 322). She is the founder of Kalakshetra and was also chosen to be a "world mother" by the Theosophical Society, but that campaign was never realized.

Rangana's disassociation from those who are unfit alludes to a notion of "vulgarity." Following the oath she recalls, her statement reflects the ideologies embedded in the founding and practice of bharata natyam as forwarded by Devi and Kalakshetra bharata natyam. Devi, with the support of several actors, including male *nattuvanars* from the devadasi community, fashioned the dance as an ancient and religious practice (while it was simultaneously revived through creative and inventive processes).[7] Thus, as Ancukam was attempting to create this ancient lineage for herself to give her body and practice legitimacy, bharata natyam, by means of Devi and the revivalists, created such a lineage through an association with text through the ancient treatises valued in Orientalist scholarship, not the lineage of the hereditary bodies who danced as devadasis. Devi moved to eradicate pervasive "vulgarity," which she believed to exist in the devadasi institution and the dance:

> Bharatanatyam is now perhaps the most popular of the Indian dances and nearly every girl in our country wishes to learn it. It is strange how far and how widely it has spread all over India. . . . [We] must pay my tribute to the professional dancers, or Devadasis for their devotion. . . . The decadence and the vulgarity that crept into the art was as much the fault of our society as theirs. (Devi Arundale 2003, 41)

The vulgarity that Devi speaks of is not isolated to the bodies of the devadasi but applies to the culture of society. To make the dance less vulgar, they framed it as no longer the dance of *sadir* in the temples and the king's court but as now bharata natyam and art, available in the proscenium theater on a secular, public stage sanctioned by what Avanthi Meduri labels "respectable people (2001, 106). This public positioning was to also answer to a perceived dissonance of dancing women in spiritual spaces of the temple. What assisted in completing the transformation of the revival was the continuous articulation of understandings of the dance by "practitioners and promoters" (O'Shea 2007, 5). Devi, in the hundreds of texts in which she was cited, brings forth her understanding, as does Rangana now—continuing to speak for what the dance should be through a sense of history that projects a notion of respectability through morality.

The public sphere as categorized and understood by the colonial and nationalist projects allowed women in Sri Lanka to access "public personas and perform roles that they may not have been able to do otherwise." (De Alwis 1997, 105). The women of Kalalaya and Saiva Mangaiyar Kalagam, ordinary yet elite, could see themselves transform society through a sense of service and intellectual pursuit, in their search for vernacular and authentic culture. Meduri states, "Ordinary men were transformed into little gods" in the nationalist movement in India (2001, 106). Here we see elite women transformed into social actors who could imagine themselves as transforming community and society against British imperialism. The social reform movement and their leaders, Navalar and Dharmapala, believed that everyday people could comport themselves differently for the sake of imperial and spiritual liberation evidenced too in the many didactic texts such as Dharmapala's "Daily Codes for the Laity" (Prothero 1995, 297).

To rid the dance form of vulgarity, Devi eliminated a swath of the repertoire from the *sadir* dance tradition, restricting performance of the dance to only those songs with *bhakti* (devotional emotion) (Meduri 1996, 270, 330). Songs of love believed to have erotic (*sringara*) elements were purged. With its different content, bharata natyam distinguished itself from the vulgar elements believed prevalent in the devadasi practice of *sadir attam* (dance). In an interview for the dance and music magazine *Sruti*, Devi states,

> Perhaps my interpretation of sringara was different from the way in which most people conceived of it. Sringara is not sensuality. It also means a love of a great kind (such as that of a godly kind). . . . But there are certain types of pada-s that I have objected to. . . . I learnt the old padam tamarasaksha (Yadhukulakhamboji) with a lot of sancari bhava-s of the languishing nayika separated from her lover. She describes not only her love but the whole process of physical contact and in gestures at that! To depict such a thing is unthinkable for me. . . . A devadasi is inured to certain things from childhood. She has seen her mother and her grandmother dance to certain things. So even if a mudra is vulgar in meaning she may not be conscious of it. But I was not brought up that way or in circumstances where vulgarity was accepted with a matter of factness. (Qtd. in Ramnarayan 1984, 23)

Devi understands not only different types of love but the cultural differences that she attributes to community, caste, and upbringing. She sees love and even vulgarity as cultural and contextual. What Devi believed to be vulgar exemplified her position as an upper-caste, upper-class woman. It was a gentility formed in part through the missionary project of colonial South Asia. In her analysis of colonial missionaries in Sri Lanka from 1820 to 1850, De Alwis shows that there was a need to "sacaralize" sex (1997, 125). Polyandry, practiced by the Kandyans, was dangerous, and even when polyandry was not practiced, missionaries interpreted Sinhala marriages to be "mere bargains," which were "contracted and dissolved with "extreme facility." Rituals such as the sharing of tobacco as a symbol of marriage were discouraged and replaced by a practice of sharing cake (De Alwis 1997, 125). Women often dressed without upper garments, so much so that the colonial project practiced the gifting of fabric and jackets. Expressions of love, sexuality, and respectability ultimately bore the marker of the influence of the colonial and missionary project. "We do not expose our body," Rangana says. The visibility of skin, so clear in Rangana's words, was not permitted in the respectable practices of Kalakshetra bharata natyam.

In the previous text Devi understood the dance to be Indian. Rangana's mother, Padma, was introduced to the form through Mahinda's father. Clearly, through Rangana's own body and that of her mother, the form traversed the borders of the modern nations of South and Southeast Asia, with women (until now) traveling to India to attend Kalakshetra. The form, through its sensibility, spoke to respectable women across religion and ethnicity. O'Shea's (2007) discussion of bharata natyam as a global form addresses how it could become pan-Indian, traversing language and religion across the subcontinent.

Rangana and Mahinda were united in their respectability as women. When we reflect on the civil war in the twentieth and twenty-first centuries, it is clear that identities and the categories by which we understand identity as scholars of Sri Lanka have shifted. John Rogers's discussion of premodern and modern Ceylon shows how the British privileged certain categories in their understanding of "true identity." Caste was immoral and incompatible with the European ideas of Buddhism, for instance. Caste was seen as a marker of the influence of Hinduism and foreign influence on Buddhism. Rogers points out that, in the centuries before British colonialism, there are examples where "a non-Sinhalese group was incorporated into caste and maintained non-Sinhalese status"; "incorporated into an existing Sinhalese caste"; or "incorporated as Sinhalese castes" and instances where religion was more or less "fundamental" to identity or where shared language did not connote shared identity across geographic regions (1994, 14–16). These locally based and European-imposed structures privilege social categories (caste, religion, language, ethnicity) differently, some fundamental and others ancillary through notions of historicity (e.g., religion) or corruption (caste). Students of those early Kalalaya years who became senior teachers and patrons, like Mahinda, learned bharata natyam *and* another form, *manipuri*, at the school. Several of the productions were arrangements between the two forms considered "Oriental."

The students at Kalalaya learned bharata natyam from a Tamil Christian teacher, Kamala Johnpillai. Despite bharata natyam's reliance on Hindu religious themes and Sanskrit texts as sources of the dance, Johnpillai expressed the universality of bharata natyam practice as taught in Kalakshetra, as shown in an interview with Roshan Peiris published in the *Sunday Observer*, two days before the "Black July" riots of 1983:

> My dancing career has taught me that all religions teach us all to
> love God. The praises sung to the divine are all the same. I worship
> the *Thipam* [lighted lamp] with devotion at a dance recital. It is all an
> expression of devotion to the Divine. Classical Dancing, and I believe all
> art forms, cut through adroitly all barriers such as creed, race and caste
> and makes us all one in our devotion to the art forms and our devotion
> to God. (1983, 9)

For Johnpillai Kalakshetra bharata natyam is a dance practice able to incorporate different faiths through its universal spiritual approach. Hindu mythology and Carnatic sounds become universal culture and a unifying force that creates its own community. Yet, when Johnpillai started teaching bharata natyam, she still experienced difference. She describes this time as situated on "virgin ground" because of a need to learn Hindu mythology and religion to grasp the form quickly. She perceived her own difference, her Christian background, as a "drawback" (Peiris 1983, 11). Nevertheless, she was still able to make a career and access a *public* professional persona—one remembered through several teachers who studied under her.

Furthermore, through the training, art is tied with spiritualism, and, although universal, there is always a sense of particular difference. The student's body considered untrained and empty is ready for cultivation, and dance becomes an intricately specific object to learn and internalize into a new subjectivity—that of the Kalakshetra bharata natyam dancer. Specific principles and movements are expected to be maintained and adhered to by its dancers, organized around the discipline of the body and the content of the repertoire, its universalism accessible through a morality of a spiritual aesthetics. The identity of a Kalakshetra student traverses other types of identity—class, religion, creed, and ethnicity—as stated by Johnpillai and Rangana. O'Shea states that the "loyalty to the school" that Kalakshetra "cultivated reveals a modern concern with individuals internalizing rules so that dancers discipline themselves." She continues,

> There is a parallel here between embodying the rules of dance, as part of dance education, and the Foucauldian (1979) paradigm of modernity in which citizens internalize discipline rather than experiencing it as submission to an outside force. Through such attention to classical principles, Kalakshetra dancers inherited a modern attention to repeatability (Franko 1989) in place of the historical priority given to the imprint of a specific mentor. This method also encouraged students to incorporate the value of Sanskrit texts so that they developed a greater loyalty to classicism than they might have if they received instruction without theoretical justification. (2007, 43)

Physical movements and choreographic strategies outside of the Kalakshetra style and its repertoire were perceived as ultimately lacking and, as Rangana criticizes, dismissive of an "oath"—an agreement rooted in reverence—that is to be upheld by the students of the institution. The perceived impropriety brought forth by dancers—those from Sri Lanka—demonstrates a form that is less concerned with the identity or nationality of those who dance it and more invested in an aesthetics accessed through outward appearance and social mores, movement, quality, and repertoire. She, in fact, fears her own shaming by her peers: "If I change my dance style, then I cannot face my teachers." Her words echo the concerns held by Mahinda's family, that dance could "jeopardize one's future." And although the form was noticeably manipulated through the process of revival, a fixity of the form emerges such that fifty years later it appears as if the dance has not changed and does not change. It becomes an "authentic form" and mirrors how identity becomes more rigid in the modern era in Sri Lanka. As Rogers states,

> Before British rule, identities were often constructed and reconstructed, both by power holders and aspirants to power. Despite many exclusivist

and some essentialist identities, there was no fully developed essentialist sociology. After British rule was established, identities continued to be constructed and reconstructed, but this process took place within a more rigid intellectual framework. It was within this framework that the twentieth-century centralization of state power and extension of the franchise led to the rise of ethnonationalism and the Sinhalese-Ceylon Tamil polarization that now dominates Sri Lankan politics. (1994, 20)

Having perceived herself as falling outside of the traditional circles of this knowledge, Johnpillai was eventually embraced within it and able to disperse the form. The form, however, requires a shift, an internalization that requires discipline, a rigidity of movement, and a belief in movement as faith, morality, and selfhood. This "category of identity," to borrow from Rogers (1994), one of the "bharata natyam dancer," can traverse other forms of identification and may be privileged in different contexts.

Although Rangana's mother is recalled by the practitioners as remarkable for the social categories of Buddhist and Sinhala, she didn't speak of Buddhism or ethnicity, only of Kalakshetra bharata natyam, with me. This was unlike the ease in which Tamil teachers discussed Tamilness and ethnicity with me, a sense of pride in the continuing of dance in spite of the current circumstances of war, a sense of pride that Tamil people had gone so far in terms of distance, only to return to their living room exemplified through my own transnational Tamil body. The conversation with Rangana avoided such discussions. My desire to be respectable was seen in my everyday outfit, as I wore *salwar khameez* with *dupatta*, earrings, and bangles and ensured my hair was tied back away from my face. I was a perpetual student in my ethnographic role, meeting with dance teachers and being asked about my dance training and my connections to Sri Lanka. My questions were strategic, building affirmation of their work as I inquired about their own journeys. But this inquiry was mired in a notion of respectability: it was not a curious inquiry that might cause trouble (hooks 2008). It was polite. It was understanding what Rangana said about covering bodies, which I did through my own dance background, my community, and my upbringing. It explained my dress that day in her living room.

The All-Ceylon Dance Festival of 1950

*Culture-as-sign articulates that in-between moment when the rule of
language as semiotic system—linguistic difference, the arbitrariness of the
sign—turns into a struggle for the historical and ethical right to signify.*
—Bhabha (1992, 49)

"What are you doing exactly, my dear?"

"I'm studying bharata natyam practices in Colombo."

"Bharata natyam is an Indian dance form. Indians do bharata natyam. We
have nothing to do with bharata natyam. Instead, our focus is on our dance,
Sri Lanka's dance is called Kandyan dance. I am curious as to why you are
working on bharata natyam. Wouldn't you go to India to study that? Where
are you from?"

The conversation was soon over, as my interest in bharata natyam convinced this teacher that I had no reason to engage with Kandyan dance
and her Kandyan-based contemporary dance company. Her claiming that
I needed to "go to India" to study the form was part of a rhetoric that had
seemed reminiscent in all countries that *I* call home, which wish to relegate
me to another place that *they* call my home. An understanding of bharata
natyam as Indian in source and practice exemplifies a specific postcolonial
condition of the form. Ignoring the noticeable presence and popularity of
the form in Sri Lanka, undone through this rhetoric is the possibility of
Sri Lanka as a site for contemporary practice, the long-standing practice
of the dance in this country I was uncovering, and the creation of markers
of nationhood.

Mahinda, the president of Kalalaya, gave me a scrapbook started by her
parents and now maintained and kept by her. The large scrapbook, with a
green cover—worn and frayed—was treated delicately in its handling, kept
wrapped in a lightweight cloth. It was filled from page to page, corner to
corner. Edges of newspaper clippings slipped beyond the edges of the book,
and I could feel the thinness of the materials, their weight worn through
the years, on the verge of disintegrating between my fingers. The papers
inside were fading into a yellow-brown shade. Some clippings lost their at-
tachments to pages with the worn glue; they were slipping in and out and
required an attentive reader to ensure they were kept and not lost. It was
there that I first saw the All-Ceylon Dance Festival. It was included in the
scrapbook as a memory for the family; the oldest daughter was featured in
the festival.

Newspaper clipping about the 1950 All-Ceylon Dance Festival in Mahinda's scrapbook.
Photo by the author.

By November 1950 dance had become such a popular form for Sri Lanka
that a national platform was created through the first All-Ceylon Dance Festival. Bharata natyam had also risen in practice and was featured in the festival, included in the category of Oriental Dance, a testament to a ubiquitous
term, with little critique, internalized in the object of Orientalists' desires.
Several of the Indian classical dance practices were included under the term
Oriental—bharata natyam, *manipuri*, *kathak*, and *kathakali*—concealing, in
current critique of Orientalist discourse, the other forms included in the two
other featured categories of Western and Kandyan, forms also entangled
with Orientalist epistemologies ("Finalists" 1950; Iyer 1950; P. Srinivasan
2011). The categories of Oriental and Western were open to women, whereas
the Kandyan category featured only men. Mahinda's sister, Neela, won first
place in the Oriental category with her bharata natyam performance, ensuring the event's inclusion in the scrapbook and her presence noted in newspapers that I would find in the government archives later.

Included under "All-Ceylon," the label *Indian*, like *Oriental*, implicated a
distance between bharata natyam and Sri Lankan culture and communities,
labeling it as unequivocally foreign. Accepting bharata natyam dance under

the term *indigenous* allowed the dance to be accepted as a product of local culture and peoples within Sri Lanka. This had a great impact on organizations like Kalalaya. In the early years the Tamil Women's Union was able to secure their space through a hundred-year lease. These different classifications—Indian, Oriental, and indigenous—had political, material, and affective implications; they distinguished a sense of belonging increasingly critical in the emerging postcolonial state. Another term was applied to the form, *Tamil*, to justify a unique experience in Sri Lanka that would exemplify a historical presence and a traditional epistemology, necessary as a foundation of nationalism and an updated response to the social reform movement of Navalar.

Oriental was a term in circulation. In 1949 the Kalalaya School of Music and Dance produced a work labeled as an "Oriental ballet," *Theva Gnana Nadanam* ("Ceylon Causerie" 1951). From a photograph clipped from an unnamed source, the dance features mudras and leg positions in certain *adavus* (basic steps) of bharata natyam. Two other works produced by Kalalaya, *Sakthi* and *Rhythm of Life* in 1950 and 1951, respectively, were also termed Oriental. *Sakthi* was described as an "Oriental dance drama" of four episodes that included themes of "feminine virtue" from the *Mahabharata* and Kannagi of the *Sillapathikaram*. The production featured both *manipuri* and bharata natyam ("Oriental Dance-Drama" 1950). *Rhythm of Life* was performed for Uday Shankar, a premier Indian dancer who gained prominence in the West ("Rhythm of Life," n.d.; Erdman 1987). *Rhythm of Life* also invoked Orientalist images: the production was described as "ballet in six scenes, depicting in dance form a day in the simple life of a village in ancient India—the utter joy of living that only a village has as its heritage" ("Art Clear," n.d.). Sri Lankan dance practitioners were Orientalizing Indian life and arts.

Although the category of Oriental was used in the festival, the press would ignore its usage and immediately label the dance as "Indian," unconcerned with the inclusion of Indian culture under "All-Ceylon." Yet the word choice also brought these forms back to political and geographic borders of modern nation-states. E. Krishna Iyer, a major figure in the revival of bharata natyam, was brought from Madras to judge the bharata natyam performances. And while in Sri Lanka, Iyer (1950) wrote about the dance as Indian and part of an "Indian tradition" and viewed India as the guide for Sri Lanka's development of the dance form.

The usage of "Indian" was unexpected to me so soon after the lifting of a law that forced so many Indians to "go home." A 1947–49 statute had disenfranchised Malaiyaha Tamils, or those that would be distinguished as

"Indian Tamils" in the English-language literature. Malaiyaha Tamils had been brought over as plantation laborers under British colonialism from 1820 to 1946, with as many as 854,800 laborers brought over by the British government in 1931. Christopher Guilmoto states,

> This trend [to limit migrations to Sri Lanka] continued until the end of the second world war, and the brief acceleration which followed was quickly limited by the policies of the newly-independent governments, especially that in Colombo which wanted to get rid of a community of foreign origin which in 1946 represented more than 11.6 per cent of the resident population of the island. Immigration was broken off completely in the 1950s and official hostility towards the Indian Tamils, who remained stateless after Independence, went on increasing. The crisis finally led to an inter-governmental agreement between Indian and Sri Lanka, signed in 1964, which provided for the repatriation to India of almost two-thirds of the population of Indian ancestry. (1993, 114)

Those that stripped Malaiyaha Tamils of citizenship were prominent Tamil politicians, such as G. G. Ponnambalam, the patron of the temple in which Ancukam worked. Other prominent Tamil political leaders, such as S. J. V. Chelvanayakam and his Tamil opposition Federal Party, opposed this move (A. Wilson 1988). In an article published during his visit as a judge for the All-Ceylon Dance Festival, Iyer stated,

> "When Ceylon is apparently set on driving out as many Indians as possible from her soil, how is it you are found visiting that country frequently?" asked a friend of mine, who had come to know of my four visits there within three years. . . . Yes, not withstanding such bickerings between the two countries, which may after all be superficial and temporary, Ceylon seems to be conscious of her close kinship with India in art and culture and to need and welcome cooperation and help from her great neighbor in the development of her arts. (n.d.)

Iyer's (n.d) ability to be facetious with his friend's remark amplifies how statelessness was far removed from his own experience. His affluence and position allowed him mobility to move across the border on request; and the arts, and its audience and participants, were privileged groups that were seen with little suspicion and permitted freedoms in contentious times. Iyer illuminates a paradox, however: while political parties were unwilling to grant the Indian Tamils citizenship, Indian arts practices flourished on a public national stage. These political parties were in disagreement, demonstrating differences in their identity. His words also demonstrate a debate in the political sector, one that took place between Tamil political parties and with non-Tamil, majority Sinhala parties. The "bickering" to which Iyer alludes had been one that some scholars state was taking place alongside the social reform movement of the late nineteenth and early twentieth centuries, gaining such force that by the midtwentieth century, it was legitimized in the political arena. The Buddhist reformer Angarika Dharmapala stated,

> We must learn to stand on our own legs and not depend on the alien. We must revive our industries, give work to our country men first before we feed the distant Austrian and Belgian who supply us with his manufactures. . . . Tamils, Cochins, Hambankarayas are employed in large numbers to the prejudice of the people of the island—sons of the soil, who contribute the largest share. (qtd. in Roberts 1978, 365)

Dharmapala equates the sons of the soil with Sinhala—Ceylon and Sinhala were synonymous—but his religious view was not as popular as secular ones in the first half of the twentieth century. Until the midtwentieth century "Sinhala nationalism was on the defensive," Michael Roberts argues, until opposition to the English-educated "class" pushed forward for a desire of "distributive justice" for the "underprivileged," which was "interlaced with the material wants of a Sinhalese sectional nationalism reaching out for shares in the economic pie" (1978, 366). Furthermore, the unity of all Tamil peoples under any political party was weak and speaks to distinction of Tamil people based on caste, class, and even geography and home on the island. Rogers (1994) observes that before colonialism, Tamil communities had very limited communication across regions.

Subsequent to the 1950 All-Ceylon Dance Festival, the dance form was, surprisingly, recognized as "indigenous." As a result of the success of the festival, the national government's Department of Education allocated 50,000 rupees to the advancement of "indigenous dancing," and bharata natyam was included under this term ("Indigenous Dancing," n.d.). However, the indigenous people of Sri Lanka, the Wanniya Laeto, have often been referenced through a misnomer as the "Vedda" and have been dispossessed of lands and suffered discrimination (in experiences often held separate from the narrative of the civil war). In Tamil culture the indigenous peoples were, as those of "untouchable castes," considered unchaste and of lowered status (Pfaffenberger 1981). Yet, in this usage, the term *indigenous* didn't have the caste association that would have been rejected. It instead gave a sense of belonging and home that was clearly becoming more critical by midcentury.

The terms *Indian* and *indigenous* were social categories of identity placed at opposing poles of the political spectrum in Sri Lanka. The term *Indian* was used in political discourse to discount belonging and the right to remain in the country. It was used to label something and someone as foreign with fewer privileges from the state. It was included among other terms that elicited a sense of "alien"-ness, like "invader" and "immigrant" (Pfaffenberger 1994, 22). *Indigenous*, on the other hand, is a category of privilege in the nation. It bestows belonging. When the Indian Tamils first arrived as laborers through British colonialism in 1820, Sri Lankan Tamils who were already on the island were compelled to create a new conception of themselves as a unique people "indigenous" to the island (Guilmoto 1993; Pfaffenberger 1994, 23). They continued to distance themselves from Indian Tamils in Sri Lanka and Tamils in India to develop their own identity and power in the colony and, later, in the newly independent state. Instead, they located their origins and identity in a "traditional homeland," one that produced a cultural tradition unique to Sri Lanka (Arasaratnam 1997, 302; Pfaffenberger 1981, 1145–46). Miscegenation was politically liable. Any influence and ties to culture outside the nation created risks of not belonging, exclusion, and expulsion. The rise of Tamil-centered parties in India—the Dravida Munnetra Kazhagam Party, which was sympathetic to a separate "Dravida Nadu" state—also contributed to the fears in Sri Lanka, creating what is often termed "barriers of accommodation":

> The old psychological fear of the Tamils cropped up and was assiduously cultivated—gaining a greater credibility with the advance of the D.M.K. in South India. "The problem of the Tamils is not a minority problem. The Sinhalese are the minority in Dravidistan. We are carrying on the struggle for national existence against the Dravidian majority," said a Member of Parliament in 1962. "If the Tamils get hold of the country, the Sinhalese will have to jump into the sea. It is essential, therefore, to safeguard our country, the nation, and the religion and to work with that object in mind," said the Mahanayake thero of Ramanya Nikaya in May 1967. In this sense the Sinhalese are a majority community with the fears of a minority.[8] (Roberts 1978, 367)

The Orientalist division of language groups and people through academic study took hold of the emergent political arena. Although *Oriental* was internalized through a local logic of difference between the Sinhala and the Tamil people—Aryan and Dravidian—it was a term utilized on the performing body that demonstrated an ambivalence under an umbrella of "All-Ceylon"—that encompassed the East and West. Yet the usage of *Oriental* following the event demonstrated distance.

One text in the scrapbook, placed close to the documentation of the All-Ceylon Dance Festival, was a short article, "How National Dances Became Fashionable," by Dr. W. Balendra, Mahinda's father. The photo that accompanies the article shows a young and distinguished man, with hair slicked back neatly to match the crispness of his black suit jacket, crisp white shirt, and thin black tie. I searched for the article in the archive to find more details but was unable to locate it, so the clipping remained just that—no publication and no date. But its proximity in the scrapbook to the All-Ceylon Dance Festival and its theme—national dance—encouraged me to believe its publication happened in the 1950s, an era where national dances were becoming popular in newly postcolonial states. It appears in dialogue with the state-led initiative to advance Sri Lanka's *own* national form—Kandyan dance—which was recontextualized from the Buddhist ritual called the kohomba kankariya in 1956. Susan Reed (2010) suggests that this creation of a Sri Lankan national dance was in response to the popularity of bharata natyam across South Asia, the form successfully traversing boundaries of ethnicity, religion, and emerging nations.

As a ritual form, the kohomba kankariya had a restricted purpose and setting, catering to ceremonially defined purposes. Recontextualization shifted the ritual to a public stage, but not out of any concern over a defilement of a ritual or a gendered, caste-based discrimination, as was the case with the devadasis and women temple dancers.[9] In the creation of Kandyan dance, kohomba kankariya, a late-night ritual performed only by men—similarly gendered in the understanding in the All-Ceylon Dance Festival of 1950—was feminized in movement to attract the young women and girls who were the base for the other (post)colonial forms rising across South and Southeast Asia (Reed 2010, 203). Reed shows that the dance was initially labeled "Sinhala dance." But by 1956, a paramount year in Sri Lanka with another mandate—the Sinhala-Only Act, which made Sinhala the sole official language of Ceylon (Sri Lanka)—the dance was then labeled Kandyan, masking its ethnic exclusiveness and transforming it into a national (Sinhala) form.[10]

Balendra's (n.d.) text maintains that bharata natyam was part of a greater Tamil culture, of which Sri Lankan Tamils were part:

> The nautch dancing tradition of Jaffna was maintained in spite of several abuses of the system and although the music and dance languished amongst the Tamils in Ceylon, their brethren in South India maintained and developed the art in spite of discouragement.

Balendra historically links the Tamils of Jaffna and those in Sri Lanka with the culture of bharata natyam through a sense of kinship with South India. He too reiterates a similar narrative to Devi, about the "fall" of the devadasi system, as he establishes, like others before him, a lineage to the "1500-years-old Bharata Natyam" practice by alluding to Tamil (Buddhist) literature, the *Sillapathikaram*. But in spite of this shared culture, he did not view the dance form as an exclusive "right" of Tamil people. In fact, he was the one who introduced prominent Sinhalese families to the form, like Rangana's mother, Padma, the first Colombo student to attend Kalakshetra. By looking at the dance form as not solely Indian but as part of a heritage belonging to the Tamils peoples of Sri Lanka and situating the dance as "national" through the article's title, Balendra makes the claim that the dance form is part of Sri Lankan (Ceylonese) heritage, accessed through "Tamil" historical and long-standing traditions. The linking of Sri Lankan Tamils with a greater Tamil intellectual and artistic heritage that was situated historically and located geographically would be foundational to the narrative of late twentieth-century Tamil nationalism. For him Tamils possess the "1500-years-old Bharata Natyam" and not Indians. For others, like the choreographer I spoke with on the phone, the dance is inherently Indian and not part of Sri Lanka.

This discussion highlights the negotiation of the form, the multiplicity of meanings that are ascribed to the dance, and, in tandem, the people and the nation. We see a resituating of the form in expected—the rhetoric of social reform that substantiated arguments through historical legacies and spiritual connections—and unexpected ways, accepting the form as Oriental, naming it as Indian, labeling it indigenous. Practice complicates the theories used to bolster the significance of the form to the public. In the *Location of Culture*, Bhabha states, "Cultures come to be represented by virtue of the processes of iteration and translation through which their meanings are very vicariously addressed to—*through*—an Other." Although Bhabha analyzes literature through poststructuralist theory, the "erasure" of "essentialist claims for the inherent authenticity or purity of cultures" is useful to the discussion of bharata natyam practice in Colombo (1994, 83).

The All-Ceylon Dance Festival illuminates a hybridity of Sri Lanka—Western, Oriental, Kandyan—where multiple cultural aspects were included that differ from the popular way in which Sri Lanka is read internally and externally. The transnational—exemplified in the movement between and association with India, both as brethren and foreigner—situates a political condition of Sri Lanka's self through the Other: Malaiyaha Tamils made stateless through a denial of home; the researcher who is to go to India to explore its form; and Tamil leaders justifying a sense of indigeneity in response to being excluded from "sons of soil." Bharata natyam is in translation through these political discourses, creating multiple meanings that rub against, contradict, and meld to shape experience, such as pride for Mahinda's family, exemplified in the maintenance of a personal scrapbook devoted to the form. Yet it is an experience that speaks to a shifting political condition. The self, through these contradictory named actors such as Dharmapala and Balendra and countless unnamed choreographers and dancers, shows the "strategy of identification" as a "response to other questions of signification and desire, culture and politics" (Bhabha 1994, 83).

Image and fantasy of the self and Other through the colonial and postcolonial imbue the form with a condition that doesn't find a resolution of the colonial presence. "Over determined from without," the identity of bharata natyam is woven into fantasies of exclusion, desires of association, and impressions of material presence and fraught absence. The dance practice is a transgressive modality "on the borders of history and the unconscious," ultimately navigating a civil conflict that is on the horizon and present at the same time (Bhabha 1994, 61).

Balendra's desire for bharata natyam to be understood as Tamil *and* to be accepted as Sri Lankan exemplifies the intellectual and choreographic tension surrounding the form, situated on a border of identification—of *this* place or *that* place—and temporal, of *that* time or *this* time. Although there are clear criticisms of studies of violence that rationalize essential identities and provide economics arguments (see Rajasingham-Senanayake 2005), the story of bharata natyam, thus far, illuminates strategies for self-making that are (post)colonial. What is unmade is an experience of comfort for those privileged actors confronting a sense of statelessness in their home of Sri Lanka, whether they are this ethnicity or not. Desires are exemplified through a stability of ethnicity and through a denial of the transnational, of the hybrid—to provide fixity in a political landscape that is unstable and to provide fixity through a rhetoric of war that maneuvers like a machine to fire at moving targets. Bhabha states,

> An important feature of colonial discourse is its dependence on the concept of "fixity" in the ideological construction of otherness. Fixity, as the sign of cultural/historical/racial difference in the discourse of colonialism, is a paradoxical mode of representation: it connotes rigidity and an unchanging order as well as disorder, degeneracy and daemonic repetition. (1994, 94–95)

Bhabha speaks of the stereotype in the colonial project, but in the (post) colonial, filled with fantasy of the Other and self, the stereotype can provide a sense of situatedness in a time and place that seems dangerously transient. In the pages that follow, bharata natyam verges on the condition of stereotype, one made in a (post)colonial frame, fixed in movement and in meaning. Unmade are the memories of change or agency of those actors like Devi. These are transformed to a repeated movement and legacy. Yet the form straddles this space as other actors negotiate explicitly its fixity through choreographic choice. Bharata natyam moves continuously to refashion the nation and the dancer.

The Difficulties Encountered after 1983

I would often have to tell the *tuk-tuk* driver to slow down to make the narrow turn into the road that leads up to Kalalaya. It's a small alleyway from a busy road that houses a large Buddhist academy. But if we turn into the entrance for the academy, we cannot make it to Kalalaya. If I wasn't paying attention in the backseat, the driver would roll on past. There is a small sign board on the main road. The lot on which the school sits is abundant with banana trees; shoots from young plants emerge from the earth, while the older ones return to it. A groundskeeper stays there and ensures that the property is safely kept—he is thin and seems older, but I am not certain how much older he really is. I realize as I write this that my photos are limited to the indoors. If I stopped on the main road to take photos of streets and signs, I would certainly seem suspect in this time of suspicion. I didn't want the trouble, so I write these descriptions from my own notes and memories.

Padmini is a local bharata natyam dance producer and Carnatic musician, and, after months of dancing in her productions, I was finally able to interview her. As we sat together sipping tea to discuss her latest production in which I was dancing, there was a lull in the conversation. I took the opportunity to ask an open question: "What are your feelings about the current practice of bharata natyam?" She replied after a brief moment of reflection:

> You have to accept that after '83, things changed. There were very good teachers like Subathra—Ganesan's mother—Kamala John Pillai, my sister Jayalakshmi. They produced very good shows. But after '83 riots, 90 percent of [Tamil] teachers vanished because of the situation. After that, there was a big lack during that time. And [some] dance teachers went to Jaffna. Most of the students also left. The present situation is a recent trend. The schools you hear of have just started in the last ten years.

The riots beginning on July 23, 1983, known as "Black July," are a historic turning point for Colombo and Sri Lanka. For two days mobs attacked homes and business. Predominantly Tamil neighborhoods—Wellawatte and Pettah—were burned to the ground, and in some other neighborhoods local police were found to have provided attacking mobs with a list of Tamil homes ("Tough Action Eases Rioting"). Black July compelled many Tamils—those who could—to leave Sri Lanka or to find ways to move back to safer, more Tamil areas in the country, like Jaffna. Certain neighborhoods never recovered, as Tamil families who could leave chose not to return to their homes, neighborhoods, Colombo, or Sri Lanka. As Serena Tenekoon states, soon after the 1983 riots, the notion of Tamils as Dravidians and as the "original invaders" of Sri Lanka, *not* indigenous to Sri Lanka, circulated frequently, surfacing in editorials in the major newspapers. This contemporary understanding of ethnicity was justified through an invocation of ancient history. She states,

> Past closely and constantly juxtaposed with the present. Mytho-historical details were not important in and for themselves but as antecedents or models for the understanding of present events. History was a mode of discourse which both facilitated and framed the discussion of ethnic relations in general and Sinhala identity in particular. (1990, 209)

Black July was preceded and followed by episodes of violence that were not solely directed at Tamils but at Muslims and Sinhala peoples as well. Most recalled episodes were the anti-Tamil riots of 1977 and 1983, the burning of the Jaffna Public Library in 1981, and a violent crushing of a Sinhala

Classes taking place at Kalalaya. Photo by the author.

youth antistate uprising in the south from 1987 to 1989. Prior to independence there was the anti-Muslim riots of 1915 and a state of emergency declared in 1958 after anti-Tamil riots. This is only a shorthand list; violence was continuous, even throughout the Cease-Fire Agreement, which was signed in 2002 but fell apart unofficially by 2007. Violence persisted in varied forms and was responded to with active dissent and critical resistance along with silence, acceptance, and a need for survival immersed in a hope for time to shift the circumstances. As I write this list, I am weary of essentializing ethnicity, of simplifying violence as identity-based, of again recounting clearly named moments that are remembered when there are countless other acts that are too many to share here and so many that are not part of the archive to which I have access.

Kalalaya was closed for ten years following Black July. Located in the prestigious area of Cinnamon Gardens and serving an affluent Tamil community, the school was left with few remaining patrons, students, or teachers. The wealthy community that it served was, for the most part, able to seek shelter abroad. The building remained but was no longer a site for events or classes. To reopen the organization, older students and graduates of Kalalaya assisted by offering classes in their own homes on behalf of the school. The school continues to survive through a system of patronage and sponsorship. Senior women provide private donations to keep the school open. The number of students it attracts or the number of audience members that attend its shows cannot financially maintain the school. The school benefits from a ninety-nine-year charitable lease granted by the government in its early days.

But in the years leading to the end of the war, dancers with whom I had the opportunity to perform with spoke of how Cinnamon Gardens was not a "Tamil neighborhood" like Wellawatte and that many Tamils were hesitant to travel to the school when they could instead easily take classes in their own neighborhoods. There was a fear of being stopped by the security checkpoints, as the school's proximity to national monuments — Independence Hall or the famous Bandaranaike Memorial International Convention Hall — meant that the surrounding neighborhood was heavily guarded by military personnel. The riots and continual violence shifted not only the perceptions of the geographic terrain of Colombo, distinguishing safe neighborhoods from unsafe ones, but also the dancing community through the exodus of dance teachers. Riots also substantially changed the meaning of the dance practice for practitioners. The experiences of riots, like the experience of institutional, national, and social exclusion; the threats of statelessness; and the imposition of the colonialism, inscribed the dance form with significance as a uniquely Tamil cultural practice, reflective of the Tamil people, their contributions to the state, and their survival in the circumstances of war and rising Sinhala nationalism.

I had the opportunity to perform at Kalalaya School of Music and Dance's annual Navarathri concert, a program that features works by both the Carnatic music and bharata natyam students of Kalalaya.[11] The open layout of the dance space was transformed into an auditorium, with chairs lined in rows filled with students' families and small lights adorning the entranceways. Kulendran, a retired professor of bharata natyam and Carnatic music, gave the keynote speech. She discussed the ways in which bharata natyam is part of Tamil culture. She connected the contemporary dance form to the dance traditions of the classical Tamil text — the same one alluded to by Balendra, the *Sillapathikaram* from the third century CE, where a devadasi, Maathavi, gives her *arangetram*, or debut performance, before the king and other noted guests. In her speech she also mentioned the dancing women in Sangam literature, a Tamil literary period from fourth century BCE to second century CE, referring specifically to the reference of *virali* and *viral vallabam kattum*, or artists who perform hand gestures. Kulendran urged the young students, mostly young girls, to be diligent in maintaining their cultural practices and identity. She found inspiration through the Indian nationalist Mahatma Gandhi:

Let the windows of my mind be open
Let the wings of culture blow through from all directions
But, let me not be swept off my feet by any.

At the end of her address, she urged the young performers to understand the beauty of Tamil culture and to "not lose" their "way," while she invoked the words of a globally recognized Indian icon—and anticolonial activist—to support her wishes. Kulendran reified the necessity for the connections between Tamil culture and bharata natyam to be maintained. Her statement connected to the cultural loss that shaped the social reform movement, the formation of Tamil cultural organizations like the Ceylon Tamil Women's Union and Saiva Mangaiyar Kalagam, and the transformation of bharata natyam into a uniquely Tamil art. Soon after the program Mahinda privately said to me, "Sri Lanka is a multicultural society."

Bhabha states, "The postcolonial perspective resists the attempt of holistic forms of social explanation. It forces a recognition of the more complex cultural and political boundaries that exist on the cusp of these often-opposed political spheres" (1994, 173). Although there is a tendency to juxtapose Kulendran's speech to Mahinda's words, I theorize connection rather than disjunction. Kulendran's words, like the circulating arguments of nationalism, cite an argument of identity through antiquity, recalling those ancient Tamil literary texts as a legacy of Tamil culture, of Tamil presence. Like the actors cited earlier, she connects Tamilness to bharata natyam. Her invocation of Gandhi's words may appear as a request for a superficial sense of "open"-ness and for those external influences of culture, outside of Tamilness, to "blow" over—while one remains steadfast, unmoved. But, through her body, the postcolonial emerges. She not only asks for a sense of rootedness but recognizes journey—a "way"—that identifies the individual in movement. She illuminates a tension between the conception of stable self, the I—identity—and transformation through the opportunity of journey. Her warning against this losing seems significant to me, in Kalalaya, which continues to be a place on the verge of being lost—one that is overlooked, unknown, and missed so often.

Kulendran's invocation of Gandhi is doubly meaningful. Gandhi is a figure whose life and afterlife continues to be associated with improper, exclusivist forms of Hindu nationalism that draws from practices of historical essentialism deployed, too, in the argument of bharata natyam as exclusively Tamil. Yet Kulendran's invocation of this figure also appears to be a sense of resistance. Here she's able to cite someone across the modern, national border—someone non-Tamil—as a source of inspiration and knowledge. This act in itself stands against the insular practice of nationalism, which denies the transnational and blocks translation. Her citation of Gandhi, not as a source of Tamilness, is a reflection of openness. Those "wings of culture" that blow over her are transformative, changing her and allowing her to change others. This act of citing a known Indian, in time of nationalism, where such transnational influences are symbols of cultural weakness, is instead a marker of a culture that changes and moves and is influenced.

Mahinda's invocation of multiculturalism may appear as a desire for state-sanctioned recognition of diversity that isolates culture, but I read it, for now, through her own body. As one of the first students of the form, Mahinda witnessed the diversity of the form, accepted as a worthy Sri Lankan dance practice across ethnicity and religion. Hers is a warning to not lose sight of *this* past and to remember her own experience of comradery across differences, once the norm and safe.

Bhabha asks in "Freedom's Basis in the Indeterminate": "How does the deconstruction of the sign, the emphasis on indeterminism in cultural and political judgment, transform our sense of the subject of culture and the historical agent of change?" (1992, 49). The sign of bharata natyam demonstrates an indeterminate, just as the war was predicted as never-ending and unwinnable. We see the weighing and constant navigation of dance and identity—not simply relativist but uneven, one that is not still but moving. It provides a sense of instability, and unknown, as it is tethered to lives and experiences lived or imagined in the past and to wished-for existence in geographies, places, and people that are desired to survive in the future.

2

Public Aesthetics, Public Education
The Role of the State in Art Education

In 1972 the Sri Lankan government conceived itself as a vital patron of the arts in the country and employed the education system to develop, encourage, and maintain specific visual and performing arts practices. The then minister of education, H. H. Bandara, believed that government support of arts would ensure that artists maintain creativity and produce work. In his report compiled for the United Nations Educational, Scientific, and Cultural Organization, *Cultural Policy in Sri Lanka*, Bandara described the "state machinery for cultural action in Ceylon." He situated government patronage of the arts historically by citing precolonial kings as the foremost patrons of the arts and proposed that the 1972 educational reforms reflected the adherence to historical tradition by the modern postcolonial government (1972, 10).

The educational reforms created a common curriculum in the public schools and developed the mandatory subject "aesthetics"—an umbrella term for visual arts, music, and dance practices—among other mandatory subjects such as science, language, and math. The reforms established the Ministry of Education as the administrator for teaching aesthetics in public schools as well as in the three government colleges—the Government Colleges of Art and Art Crafts, of Dance and Ballet, and of Music—now included within the University of Visual and Performing Arts in Colombo. The curricula incorporated the reconstructed and revived dance forms that were recognized markers of indigenous practices by the mid-twentieth century; the requirement for learning aesthetics was a means of postcolonial nation building, as a tool of cultural recovery and as a response to development mandates in education required by foreign donors. Like Kalalaya and Saiva Mangaiyar Kalagam—the organizations discussed in the previous chapter—the state's interest in teaching local arts was a means of "undoing" a colonial psyche. Aesthetics was, however, conceived as cultural knowledge rooted in the local and *not* foreign, despite the investment of foreign monies in education and in the state and the framework of free and public education built under a colonial era. In the overview of the cultural policies in Sri Lanka provided for UNESCO, Bandara observes,

> It has been pointed out by Ananda Coomaraswamy that, those who . . . perceive how the religious, artistic and national life of the people formed together the expression of one culture which all classes shared, will understand how impossible it was that the arts should continue to flourish under foreign rulers ignorant of, and in the main opposed to, the perpetuation of that culture and religion. (1972, 11)

With Coomaraswamy, Bandara notes that the arts had a communal and national frame in the charge of creating "one culture" to represent all peoples. Bandara situates his approach among other postcolonial countries, which, "in addition to winning of political freedom and a total measure of self-government, carried many an undertone of cultural revival" (1972, 12). Here Bandara celebrates these revived forms and sees the state as independent of its colonial status—it is free and liberated. My interest is to complicate Coomaraswamy's notion of "one culture," not only critiquing this idea for its nationalist sentiments but analyzing what "one culture" is (or what many cultures are) possessed by the state and how such possession of revived or recontextualized forms finds support through neoliberal movements and authoritarian structures. Bandara uplifts the state for its important work in maintaining artists *outside* of the market:

> The role of the State in the development of culture, as far as Ceylon is concerned, is something that has been accepted as a matter of course. . . . It is not the belief in Ceylon that the arts develop when they are "starved" of direct official patronage, or that "poverty stimulates creativity" and is therefore a blessing in the long run. The artist has always relied more or less on State support as one of his fundamental rights which the State was obliged to grant. (10)

In this analysis I ask, how does the aesthetics requirement merge nationalism with neoliberalism?

This chapter discusses how, in theory and practice, the aesthetics requirement interweaves neoliberal developments in the Sri Lankan economy with state-governed education, acting as a junction between cultural nationalism and political neoliberalism. I argue that aesthetics is a type of development project for the postcolonial nation, weaving cultural nationalism with neoliberal developments that are mandated through foreign aid and a government's response to local insurgencies and demands of the citizenry. Adding to the discussion from the last chapter regarding ethnicity and identity and dance, I continue to explore the interweaving of individual, communal, and national identity and the arts and consider how women's bodies are the primary site for this type of development. Embodiment of identities and of neoliberal development through arts practice is considered and accessed through ethnography.

In discussing the connection between identity and economics, I am emboldened by the work of Sri Lankan and South Asian diasporic scholars who critique the tendency to separate ethnic identity from economic analysis when speaking of Sri Lanka and its civil war. Ahilan Kadirgamar argues that the focus on ethnicity as explanations for the war diminished critical economic studies and the ways in which money factors into people's experiences alongside how finances feature in the government's handling of the war (2017, 11). Darini Rajasingham-Senanayake points out that "economically rational" explanations also share a "common intellectual heritage with colonial modes of representation of 'other' cultures and their violence, including essentialist ethnic explanations" that privilege "primordial" explanations (2005, 552). This chapter continues to trace the developments of the aesthetic mandate to understand how cultural nationalisms intersect with (economic and embodied) development and neoliberalism. In light of this investigation, it is worth quoting Radhika Desai as a starting point for this intersectional analysis:

> The political economy of cultural nationalisms was typically neoliberal—flagrantly unequal and not primarily concerned with increasing production or productivity so much as with the enrichment of the (expanded but still tiny) dominant middle, propertied and capitalist classes. The new nationalisms' cultural politics—whether conceived in religious, ethnic or cultural terms—conceived culture as static, pre-given, and original although, amid the intensified commercialism and commodification of neoliberal capitalism, it was less so than ever before, and attributed to it almost magical powers of legitimation and pacification over potentially restive forsaken majorities. Thinking of cultural nationalisms as majoritarian and homogenizing is easy, but also mistaken: for in the neoliberal context, cultural difference—different levels of competence in and belonging

to the national culture—served to justify the economic inequalities produced by neoliberal, market-driven policies. Cultural nationalisms often took apparently multicultural and "tolerant" forms as markets performed the work of privileging and marginalization more stealthily and more effectively. (2008, 400)

As discussed in the previous chapter, nationalisms' cultural politics were invested in a constructed form of tradition, one that denied its hybrid existence and clearly invested the (social and intellectual) capital that emerged from the static form of the performing arts on bodies of specific class and caste and vice versa. In looking at aesthetics, I consider, as Desai points out, the "different levels of competence" (in relation to the state) that emerge in artistic practice within the educational practice. I rely on the discussion of aesthetics by various actors within the Ministry of Education from past to 2007 (the period of my fieldwork) and by contemporary educators and scholars of education or arts to understand the ambivalent ways in which dance, and bharata natyam in particular, is included within state-managed, public, and free education.

Public Education and Public Aesthetics Education

Sri Lanka would become the first country in Asia to implement universal adult franchise in the early 1930s (although "universal" was quickly contested with the inclusion of Malaiyaha Tamils). Enfranchisement, granted in 1931, would contribute to the development of social welfare and progressive projects that followed, such as free public education (Kadirgamar 2017, 42). Public and free education was created in Ceylon in the mid-1940s, while the country was still under British colonial rule. There was widespread criticism of the British education system for the bifurcation it created between a privileged English education sector, to which access was limited, and the vernacular schools, which formed the larger sector of the school system (and, in fact, were always free) (Perera, Wijetunge, and Balasooriya 2004, 395; de Silva and de Silva 1990, 10). De Silva and de Silva state,

Perhaps the most glaring inequality, however, was between opportunities available for those who studied through the English language and the students who learned through Sinhala or Tamil. Schools in the first category were few in number. They levied fees and were thus barred to a majority of the people. This explains why literacy in English was limited to 6.3 percent of the population as late as 1946. Furthermore, secondary education was provided almost exclusively in schools that taught in English and recognized secondary education institutions proved to be an even more exclusive group. Secondary education in English led students to the legal and medical professions or to lucrative positions in government service. In contrast, the Sinhala and Tamil schools taught little beyond basic literacy skills. Thus, the education system created a privileged minority and a disadvantaged minority divided largely on the basis of the language of education. (1990, 10)

The division created by the British education system was addressed through the creation of a public education system that would be accessible to all "irrespective" of "wealth or social status" (Sri Lanka Special Committee 1943, 9). Free public education was thought of as a concept of democracy that reflected the principles held in ideal Sri Lankan nationhood (even before independent nationhood existed). The "nationhood" fostered through this "new democratic" education system would give value and priority to Sri Lanka's "traditional cultures" (10). In his vision for free education, the first minister of education for Ceylon, Dr. C. W. W. Kannangara—often cited in any text regarding Sri Lanka's public education program as the founding father of the modern, postcolonial Sri Lankan education system—strove to create a nation that educated all through its recognition of vernacular languages, religions, and cultures. His vision resulted in government schools that taught in Sinhala or Tamil. The irony was that the public education system was enacted under British colonialism and by Sri Lankan elites. In his report for UNESCO, Bandara identifies the education system as the only "cultural activity" of the independent government that was "associated" with colonial powers and argues that education, as a "cultural activity," was used to reinforce the colonial project (1972, 12). He argues that the only local cultural activities that piqued the interest of the colonial power was archaeology and artifacts, which resulted in the establishment of the National Museum in 1876 and the Department of Archaeology in 1890. In spite of the colonial history, Bandara sees education as part of the modern project of nation building. Distancing the postcolonial state from the colonial one, the postcolonial state intends to do the same.

Critiques of public and free education have persisted and continue to remain. Foremost was that it failed to remove class as a factor, that discrepan-

C. W. W. Kannangara Mawatha in Colombo, on February 4, 2009. Photo by the author.

cies still persist between urban schools and rural schools, and that the percentage of GDP spent on education has fallen over the period of the war and continues to remain minimal (Wanasinghe 1988; Kadirgamar 2015). Jayampati Wanasinghe (1988) reveals that the "center-periphery" (urban-rural) divide perpetuated by the British system remained in spite of free education reforms and led to insurgencies, including the first uprising of the Janatha Vimukthi Peramuna (JVP)—a Sinhala-based communist Marxist-Leninist party that organized around workers' rights—and emboldened Tamil resistance movements. Jonathan Spencer sees the competition model within the education system as creating persistent discriminatory measures in a language that is to benefit "the whole":

> In the 1950s competence in Sinhala became the official route into
> government employment (even though English remained the de-facto
> language of power); in the 1970s quotas were introduced to open up
> higher education to young people from relatively disadvantaged parts
> of the country. . . . In processes like this, competition for scarce state
> resources was itself experienced through key markers of identity like
> language: political economy transmuted into cultural struggle. The first

gestures of violent insurrection in the Tamil north followed closely on the introduction of so-called "standardisation" in university entrance in the 1970s. Perceptions of distributive injustice have been important sources of anti-state insurrection among both Sinhala and Tamil youth since the 1970s, but their perceptions of relative advantage and disadvantage have again been almost always structured along ethnic lines. (2008, 614–15)

The youth-led antistate insurrections that Spencer speaks of include the JVP and various Tamil youth groups that preceded or were early contemporaries of the Liberation Tigers of Tamil Eelam (LTTE). The JVP fought both of the major parties that have governed the country, the Sri Lankan Freedom Party (SLFP) and the United National Party (UNP), stating that they were both a type of "bourgeois" government who created an "economic-political-social crisis for which it had no solution" ("Brief History" 1999). The first uprising took place in 1971—the year before the educational reforms were implemented—and is said to have taken thirty thousand lives, mostly youth defeated by Sri Lanka security forces. The first insurrection was an "abortive attempt" to overthrow the then Bandaranaike (SLFP) government (Reed 2010, 18). Policy changes in education that maintained divisions in terms of ethnicity and class also emboldened the Tamil resistance movements, including the LTTE (Wanasinghe 1988, 99–100). The education reforms in 1972 appeared to respond, in part, to protests over the lack of professional opportunities for the youth (and the influence of foreign capital) and initiated a vocational-oriented educational curriculum in aesthetics that, through the arts, allowed for an identity-based multiculturalism.

Starting in grade 4, students are offered classes in several arts practices: visual arts (unspecified), music (in three different styles: Carnatic, Sinhala, and Western), and dance in two different styles (Kandyan and bharata natyam). By grade 6, when the students are eleven years of age on average, they are required to choose an arts practice in which to specialize. They then study that practice through grade 11 and have the opportunity, depending on their Ordinary-Level exam results, to write an Advanced-Level exam in the practice.[1] Passing the A-Level exam gives them the opportunity to continue their studies at the university level. In primary schools aesthetics classes are offered twice a week for twenty minutes, in secondary-level schools, forty. In the arts-focused public universities, students develop their understanding of an arts practice to gain certification, which will enable them to be hired as arts or aesthetics teachers. The certification is honored by arts organizations outside of government schools and some private schools that follow the state syllabus. It offers employment potential. The reforms established a structural relationship between the state, arts, and education.

Aesthetics were believed to develop two ideals in students: creativity and critical thinking. Kannangara stated in the 1943 *Ceylon Sessional Papers*:

> Art education has so many advantages that great emphasis should be placed on it. It trains the hand, the eye and the mind in certain specific directions. It makes one see more in the everyday things of life. It gives practice in imagining beautiful designs and pictures. . . . It gives an absorbing field for concentration. . . . The fact that the student is required to do something and not merely to know something is also of profound social significance. (Sri Lanka Special Committee 1943, 87–88)

For Kannangara arts are a unique subject in a curriculum through its development of embodied knowledge and in doing—producing. It develops a sense of critical engagement through "seeing more" in the everyday. The 1972 reforms are argued to further extend Kannangara's vision, providing for the "total" education "given" to the child (Bandara 1972, 37).

Yet the nation building that the state celebrated through Bandara's discussion of the cultural policy for UNESCO is exclusive. In spite of the "multiracial and multi-religious" qualities of Ceylonese society, Bandara prioritized what he terms are "indigenous" and the "majority" culture (1972, 9). He insists that 1956 was a landmark year for a "silent political revolution which gave the 'common man' a sense of self-importance and self-confidence. There was a definite assurance of recognizing his language and everything that was *indigenous*" (13; emphasis mine). Dance scholar Susan Reed discusses the significance of this year: a key rallying point for the SLFP was support for a language policy of "Sinhala only," making Sinhala the sole official language. This policy effectively excluded all other ethnic groups from state employment, the major source of employment in the country (2010, 134). The term *indigenous* in Bandara's usage is narrow and exclusionary, demonstrating a shift from the usage in the early to mid-twentieth century.[2] According to Bandara, 1956 was the year that the state was able to set up formal and effective machinery by establishing a Ministry of Cultural Affairs, which supported Kalayatanas that train students in North Indian classical music and local dance forms (1972, 13). Bandara argues that these practices are rooted in local and "indigenous" culture (40).[3] Bharata natyam is not mentioned at all in the report. Reed points out that after 1956, Kandyan dance received "patronage of the state" through the Ministry of Cultural Affairs and the Ministry of Education (2010, 133). Although Kandyan dance was offered in schools in the Central Province as early as the 1940s, the 1950s marked a clear difference in state sponsorship for dance.

In a report from the Ministry of Education and Ministry of Higher Education for the International Conference of Education held in Geneva in 1986, fourteen years after the implementation of the common curriculum and aesthetics as a required subject, education was to develop "attitudes conducive to the maintenance of harmonious relations among the different ethnic groups" (1986, 2). Unlike the previous document from 1972, in this document Sinhala, Carnatic, and Western types of music are mentioned, and the two subjects listed in dance practice are "Dancing" (meaning Kandyan) and bharata natyam. Alongside promoting Buddhist nationalist sentiment as a means for justifying equality and working against any discrimination within the education system, the state clearly is interested in cutting costs to education, shifting away from studies in the arts and humanities to science-based courses (in the universities) to comply with a cost-cutting recommendation set forth in the International Conference on Education, a division of UNESCO (Wanasinghe 1988, 101). Major donors to education also cited Sri Lanka's development status (poor) to argue that higher education was irrelevant for a life of productivity and economic earning in the country. As a report from the Swedish International Development Agency states, a "very poor economy simply does not require 75 percent of new entrants to the labour force to have more than a basic primary education" (Engquist, Jivén, and Nyström 1981, 17).

The aesthetics curriculum responded to and enacted discriminatory measures. Developed through state interest in the arts to provide for employment of a dancer-and-drummer community who was the source of the Kandyan form, it was also a means through which a larger base of students could learn what was constituted as a national form for employment in a context of youth discontent and political instability. The inclusion of bharata natyam—a form with a longer history of formal training and certifications (outside of the state)—was a means to demonstrate state sponsorship of minority arts and to potentially subdue ethnicity-based resistance.

Sanchari Bhava #1: Kannagasabaratnam

The setting is an office in a university campus in Colombo.[4] That day a friend of mine, Kamani, who teaches music at the University of Visual and Performing Arts, accompanied me as we visited the several campuses within the city. Her familiarity with the security guards at the campuses and her position as a lecturer helped me get into the campus grounds. Her fluency in Sinhala was extremely helpful at this campus, where the language of instruction is Sinhala.

We stopped at the University of Visual and Performing Arts looking for written materials on the aesthetics requirement, but as we walked through several departments, no one seemed to have any idea of where to find what we were looking for. We walked up and down stairs and through halls, into and out of offices; the feeling of failure grew step by step. From morning until early afternoon, we struggled to find someone to speak with about aesthetics. We decided to take an ice-coffee break at a café across the street. Our next and last stop would be the Department of Education, we decided.

Heading to the education complex, we saw signs for the "Office" and walked in. The office was narrow, with a long desk, behind which assistants were seated. Adjacent was a room full of file cabinets and students discussing materials with one another. Within a minute a smiling, middle-aged, mustached man with thick black hair, dressed in slacks and a white short-sleeved shirt, saw us. Kamani explained our mission in Sinhala. When she told him that I was a researcher from the United States, he started to speak to us in English and quickly seated us in his office. He eagerly explained his ideas on the aesthetics subject. A classic nameplate long enough to accommodate his lengthy surname sat at the front of his large wooden desk: Kannagasabaratnam. Instead of sitting behind the desk, he took a seat in front of it, and we sat on either side of him. His office was filled with papers, binders, and old, heavy furnishings. My pencil attempted to transcribe his words to paper with the same level of eagerness he carried in educating us on the school system.

Kannagasabaratnam ascribed to aesthetics a central value of promoting cultural understanding and the creation of social relationships that will lead to peace, not war. "There's no point in just focusing on 'economic' values. We have to learn how to live together; we need people, need dance, need an audience," he said. "Dance is a social activity." With its condition of hours of sharing instruction and viewing classmates and performers, dance is a social activity that often engages the participation of a larger community as instructors, supporters, and witnesses. For Kannagasabaratnam from the dance practice a sustainable peace will arise from the people, not top-down through government, treaties, or cease-fires. "Bharata natyam is a perfect example." He continued,

> Tamil and Sinhalese parents are proud of children learning this dance. A Tamil audience appreciates the learning of bharata natyam by Sinhalese girls. Their appreciation is so high. There's respect. Bharata natyam is a Tamil dance, and through aesthetics education it can have a big role in nation building by fostering an interaction among people. If I am Tamil and I sing a Sinhalese song, there's happiness. People are impressed by that knowledge.

For Kannagasabaratnam peace is based on an exchange of cultural practice, which requires interaction between peoples, participants, and audiences—across difference—and education in the arts can provide that. The knowledge and care through learning a practice are forms of labor that convey respect to that object—the dance—and to the Other, the community symbolized through that practice (whether or not they desired for it to be a symbol of their community). Kannagasabaratnam pointed out that in the first two years of its study, aesthetics provided a means for understanding the Other and oneself through the "survey" of cultural practices. As alluded to in his statements, the framing of the conflict as either economic or cultural is a common one in Sri Lanka. Concerns over economics versus cultural exchange are separated in his statement. But, as I spoke to teachers, economics was a major factor for their investment in following the curriculum within the school system; it was a reason to argue that the government supported Tamil artists.

Yet as these dances become part of national-cultural narratives, the complex and interwoven exchanges of identity through the form are replaced with knowledge of practices marked as unchanging tradition. The marker of the identity, the object-as-dance, is kept and considered a form given and replicated on different bodies. As Rangana's words showed in the previous chapter, a dance practitioner gains respect through that allegiance to past time, the specific ways of keeping this gift unchanged. The symbols of culture cited by Kannagasabaratnam—language (through the song he mentions) and dance (through bharata natyam) are positioned differently in relationship to the state. The practice of minority communities having to learn the language of the majority is plentiful in diverse and hybrid countries. The Sinhala-Only Act is a violent example of this expectation, and, although Kannagasabaratnam's example is situated within an act of individual agency with pleasure, care, and peace, the dynamics of inclusion and exclusion continue. The object of language becomes a performance for belonging. Bharata natyam, his other example, similarly is constructed as unifying marker through a kind of boundary crossing and traversing between communities. But what happens when forms dispossessed once through the modern state are dispossessed a second time through a postcolonial notion of an abstraction of art? What do these practices mean in a context of conflict and war? How does the cultural exchange of Sinhala bharata natyam differ in 2007 from that practice in the mid-1940s, when bharata natyam first emerged?

Kannagasabaratnam's suggestion that aesthetics would heal problems of ethnic difference or war in the country through mutual cultural understanding and sharing seemed questionable to me. I began to suspect his motives and wondered whether he was saying this because he works for a public university. From his name and his later exchange with me in Tamil, I felt he was trying to dismiss the difficult political barriers to peace that have brought on by the civil war. At the same time I did not know him, so why would he trust me with any truth? Trust was unavailable, and I was participating in its undoing. My suspicion of him mirrored the suspicion of another dance teacher for participating in government programs.

Sanchari Bhava #2: Ganesan

Ganesan was seated across from me, wearing a loose-fitting housecoat, comfortable and confident in her home, while I was nervous about our conversation, in hopes of impressing her enough for her to maintain communication with me. My goal in this initial conversation was to introduce myself again to her, having met her two years before, by discussing my dance training and my purpose in conducting research in Colombo. I delved into my biography—listing the places I have lived and studied—and soon into my story we found an event where our paths had crossed. "I've met you before at my student's arangetram in Calgary. Your parents loaned a Nataraja statue—do you remember? You must've been quite young then," she said with a curious smile. I remembered the arangetram but didn't realize my family's part in it, nor had I made the connection that she was onstage that day. After laughing at the notion of being in the same place at the same time almost two decades prior, she launched into her own life story, explaining in more detail her dance training and her current teaching and choreography.

The interest in my eyes must have been visible as she spoke. She wished I could attend her upcoming concerts to see the new works onstage but thought it impossible. It was well known that Ganesan was selected to choreograph a piece and present her students at the president's house in celebration of the Tamil harvest festival, Thai Pongal. The security situation was growing increasingly tense with rising hostilities between the Tigers and the Sri Lankan army. War was expected. With disappointment she told me that I would not be able to attend these performances. Their locations merited the presence of high security, which barred outside guests from entering. "That's the struggle too," she said, "We can't even invite people to see our shows because of the security situation." Thus, even her own performance—one that was to demonstrate cultural understanding and inclusion at the highest level of the country—was a private affair. Invitations on her behalf were nonexistent.

As she spoke of her participation in such a visible national and government-sponsored festivity, there was defensiveness in her tone:

> I couldn't reject the invitation from the president to choreograph for the Thai Pongal celebration. As someone well established here, I can't say "no" because then it will look like I don't support the government. But in my heart I'm sad that our people are dying and suffering. The government suspects the political allegiances of teachers coming from Jaffna. But because I'm from Colombo, they know they can trust me.

Instead of delving into these difficulties, Ganesan restricted her discussion of the current political situation to speak of the positive features of the government and dance teaching in Sri Lanka. "The best thing that this government has done was to develop an aesthetics requirement in the school," she asserted.

> More and more people are learning bharata natyam because of that. Some take to art, some to music, and some to dance, and bharata natyam is one of the subjects offered. People can sit for exams in bharata natyam. This happened in 1972. The school requires several subjects: math, English, Tamil, religion, science, and health. In addition to them students must also learn aesthetics. Aesthetics includes art,

Carnatic music, Western music, Kandyan dance, and bharata natyam. Students are required to take it from grade 6 onward, up to the A-level exams. Students can then be qualified as teachers.[5]

Ganesan was aware of the criticisms of her participation in the national program and of those lobbied against the government for its approach in the war (and the increasing surveillance of Tamil communities). Animosity toward the government was projected onto her because of her participation in the government program. Bharata natyam is a projected and *acceptable* marker of Tamilness, utilized as a sign of diversity and inclusion in Sri Lanka. It was featured as a Tamil performance for a Tamil event, and her involvement brought forth suspicion from her own community. Bharata natyam practitioners—like her—are in a difficult financial position. Opportunities to perform with financial or organizational support are limited for community artists. Her statements reflect the political divisions within the community and the ways in which allegiance and safety are intertwined with place and bodies. Tamil bodies are suspect based on geography and distance from Colombo, from the government. Ganesan's concerns for the people dying around her while simultaneously worrying about the consequences of refusing or accepting the government's demands were illuminative of the difficult positions of many artists, who were seen in the binary, either rejecting or accepting their own community, fearing the consequences of not being perceived as ambivalent toward the government or resisting it fully.

The aesthetics requirement appeared to be an employment opportunity and profitable for dance teachers. It created interest in the dance form and provided employment for dance teachers at present and in the future. But Ganesan did not mention the benefit of the aesthetics requirement as an act of implementing cultural understanding, nor the sense of creativity that was garnered through artistic practice. Her interest in aesthetics was the support by the state that ensured her stable employment as a bharata natyam teacher.

Does the aesthetics requirement promote creativity and critical thinking as declared by Kannangara, a sense of cultural knowledge as discussed by Bandara, or cultural understanding through cultural exchange as believed by Kannagasabaratnam? What was the experience for teachers of aesthetics, was it the "best thing," as Ganesan proclaimed?

Sanchari Bhava #3: Sonia

Tayum tatta tayum tam; tayum tatta tayum tam; tayum tatta tayum tam. Wearing a dark-green chiffon sari, Sonia was seated on the floor at the front of the classroom with a small wooden block at her legs. With a slender wooden stick, her left hand beat out the syllables as she said them repeatedly, "Tayum tatta tayum tam." Her right hand counted out the *tala* cycles with each finger and the flipping of the hand, while her left hand doubled and tripled the speed of the beat with the hitting of the stick.[6] I was in the last row, behind two rows of young female dancers aged five to thirteen. They were dressed in orange-and-green cotton *salwar khameez*, and their black hair was tied back in plaits or ponytails. The youngest students' hair was too short to tie, so they wore small barrettes to hold hair away from their eyes. In unison with Sonia's syllables and beats, we stepped out our right foot and then our left, trying to maintain our *aramandi* as our outstretched hands spun in unison with our leg movements and our heads turned from right to left with the beat. Sonia announced corrections to our movements and body positions.

Although I learned these steps before, I was attending Sonia's class to learn the specific Kalakshetra bharata natyam basic techniques. After correcting us through several adavus—commenting on the degree of bend at our waists, on the straightness of our backs—Sonia asked us to sit on the floor for the dance-theory lesson. The younger girls, aged four to eight, were learning the *shlokas* for the single-hand and double-handed gestures.[7] The older girls in junior high and high school were learning the head positions outlined in the *Natya Shastra*. They recited the shlokas in unison along with the movements. All of them took notes in their books, asking one another for help in remembering the new lesson. They turned in their books for correction to Sonia. The youngest girls did not know how to write down the lessons, so they did *namaskaram* and returned to their mothers, who were sitting down and chatting in the back of the rehearsal space.[8] I waited for Sonia to dismiss the rest of the class, and when she did I sat next to her with my recorder and microphone.

Sonia is one of many dance teachers who teach bharata natyam in the government schools in Colombo; she also teaches two classes at a community school in the city. We are close in age and initially met dancing in a bharata natyam performance troupe for a television program. As I learned from her in the class and danced with her in rehearsal, she occasionally mentioned issues teaching dance at the school. I told her that I would be interested in hearing more of her concerns, and she agreed to discuss them with me for this research. However, that day, as I sat with her, she was hesitant to indulge in speaking about her grievances with teaching aesthetics "for the record."

Instead of pressing her about those grievances, I asked for her thoughts on the potential for cultural understanding through the learning of aesthetics. Sonia told me that classes in aesthetics are segregated by the language medium, as most classes are, even within the same school. After the nationalization of schools and the switch to teach in *swabhasha*—the local languages—the segregation by language and, inherently, ethnicity became more prominent (Perera, Wijetunge, and Balasooriya 2004, 396). Sonia pointed out that even though bharata natyam is introduced to all students, most Sinhala students choose Kandyan dance when they are asked to choose a form:

> I'm teaching only Tamil students. In grades 4 and 5, small girls come from [the] Sinhala medium [classes]. They don't learn more than simple things, like *tatta adavu*. From grades 6 to 11, I teach only Tamil students, because they [the Sinhala students] have their Kandyan dance and their music.[9]

Although there is an effort made to share different aesthetic disciplines with the students in the first two years of the program, the segregation of students by language medium does not break boundaries of language. It focuses on the learning of a form from the teacher but is not invested in building social relationships between students from different language mediums. Reed (2010) points out that prior to the 1972 reforms and as early as the 1940s, Kandyan dance was already encouraged in several schools and enforced more widely in 1956. By the time Sonia and I were speaking in 2007, it seemed there was a perpetual unevenness in the availability of Kandyan and bharata natyam dance teachers across all schools, and this limited any possible exposure to many styles within the educational system. According to the curriculum, students are supposed to learn several subjects within aesthetics (Western and Hindustani music, visual arts, Kandyan dance, and bharata natyam) in grades 4 and 5, but they are offered classes in those disciplines only if there are teachers hired to teach them. It was not a requirement for every school to offer both forms, and none of the Tamil-medium schools offered Kandyan dance, while some Sinhala-medium schools offered both bharata natyam and Kandyan dance.

In addition, the syllabus and examinations for Kandyan dance and bharata natyam are not available in both Tamil and Sinhala. The syllabus for bharata natyam dance is based on the North Ceylon Oriental Music Society, a separate examination board based in Jaffna. It was integrated within the state curriculum with the aesthetics requirement. Similarly, the Kandyan dance syllabus appears based off the exams and curriculum of a private organization, Lanka Gandharva Sabha, whose aim was to popularize North Indian classical music and Kandyan dance (Reed 2010, 141). For students who are seeking Ordinary- and Advanced-Level qualification in dance studies, the choices are obvious: one can pursue only the dance that gives an exam in the language medium in which they are educated. Exams in bharata natyam are available only in Tamil, and exams in Kandyan dance are available only in Sinhala. The writing of Ordinary- and Advanced-Level examinations in dance is a driving force behind pursuing aesthetics in dance because it provides future professional opportunities. Although she did not believe that students must be limited to the cultural practice associated with their identity, Sonia viewed the choice as meaningful and practical.

Teaching opportunities are contingent on the writing of both the Ordinary- and Advanced-Level exams. The exams structure the entire syllabus of aesthetics, standardizing the material taught and learned. The standardization of the dance includes a fixed syllabus, which must be adhered to. This syllabus specifies which adavus and dance compositions are taught from year to year. Since the syllabus is standardized, all the teachers have to teach the same items. In the first two years, grades 4 and 5, students are exposed to various basics of several practices. According to the bharata natyam syllabus, in grade 6, students learn the first two groupings of adavus (*tatta* and *natta*). The grade 7 syllabus requires the teachers to teach two more groupings, *ta tai tai ta* and *tat tai tam* (also called *mai* and *korvai*). During grades 8 and 9 they complete learning all the adavus. The syllabus for grade 10 requires students to learn the *alarippu* and jatiswaram, the first two items in a traditional *margam* repertoire.[10] In grade 11 students are taught *sabdam*, the third item in the margam format.

Even with the items taught during the last two years of the aesthetics, it appears that teachers are limited as to what specific pieces they can teach. Teachers are given two jatiswaram songs and two *sabdam* songs from which to choose.[11] Those pieces too must incorporate certain adavus, *abhinaya*, and mudras as assigned in the syllabus.[12] Thus, each year, more or less, the teachers teach the same thing with little chance for innovation within the classroom and little chance for self-expression by either the teachers or the students. One of Sonia's main criticisms of the aesthetics syllabus was that it was repetitive. She was able to tap into her creative talents with less restriction than when she was asked to coordinate, choreograph, and program school wide concerts *outside* of teaching aesthetics.

The aesthetics syllabus is repetitive not only for teachers but for students as well. Many students start learning dance outside of their school and are familiar with the syllabus materials prior to engaging with them through the school. Aesthetics classes become a review of basic steps and pieces already learned. The program becomes an exposure to the syllabus as taught in the school; it gives an introduction to the teaching methodologies necessitated in the aesthetics program. The outcome of the familiarity of the content is that aesthetics courses are not considered serious subjects in which students must apply themselves and study to grasp new content. In terms of bharata natyam practice, what they learn in their years of study in aesthetics is typically learned in the first three years of classes with a private teacher—it is quite elementary.

Creativity, a value ascribed to the learning of aesthetics by Kannangara, is not foregrounded in the practice of aesthetics education. Bandara warned against this very situation, in which artists, as teachers, were not asked to incorporate their creative talents in their professional positions but instead sacrifice creativity in the interests of professionalization. He states, "It is not surprising that the first concern of any student learning these arts is employment as quickly as possible. . . . But, it's important that they maintain creativity" (1972, 41). The exams in bharata natyam are based on memorization of the material, not on creatively reading or dancing it. They do not incorporate analytic readings of theory, nor require composition in terms of practice.[13] The syllabus locates knowledge in the dance as a memorization of both its theory and its disciplinary practice. Practical knowledge tests the students' execution of technique or the basic vocabulary in bharata natyam consisting of adavus, combinations of adavus, and the verbal syllables (*sollukattu*), along with several shlokas and their meanings. Theory knowledge, in essence, tests the students' memory of adavu names, adavu groupings, mudras, and body movements.

Aesthetics becomes a form of discipline of the body and of the mind, the repetitive practice that trains the body for postcolonial nation building through national dance (Kandyan) and represented dance (bharata natyam). The body memorizes form, repeats it in a slow and limited manner, and is expected to learn content to re-create that same framework, even if one knows beyond what is asked. The Swedish International Development Agency stated in 1981, "The whole education system can be said to suffer from what has been termed the diploma disease. The system is ingrained with examinations, which disturb learning and training, and the lack of certification may very well debar a student from employment" (Engquist, Jivén, and Nyström 1981, 17). A high level of education was not necessary for a poor economy. And so, in the same publication for the same fiscal year, the agency provided 13 million Swedish kroner (approx. US$2.7 million in 1981) in support of an education system directed toward "practical and technical subjects at the secondary level, viz home economics education, agricultural science and handicraft subjects" (ii). As Sri Lanka put the onus on the colonial governments for its present-day conflict, Sweden found a means to criticize Sri Lanka for a culture of certification as it continued to promote such programs.

The mandatory requirement and the creation of certification was routed in nation building that took place before the implementation of a common core curriculum in 1971—it was modeled on certifications developed in other arts schools in the country. Reed states,

> In 1936 the Gandharva Sabha, a private organization, was established in order to promote the study of North India, South Indian, and Kandyan dance and music. Although private, the Gandharva Sabha was instrumental in establishing standards for the credentialing of dance teachers for the government schools. In fact, according to one of my consultants, Mr. H. M. A. B. Herath, the motive for introducing formal exams for dance and music came from Mr. Kapukotuwa, who wanted to provide a means for the traditional dancers and musicians to qualify for government teaching appointments, as they did not have the usual educational credentials. (2010, 116)

The formalization of the curriculum was to provide certain economic classes and communities access to the state for earning income and stability. At the same time their students' work and their bodies' integration into the state apparatus continuously dispossessed the form from its traditional community, learned and replicated by those outside of it.

As the ministry was designing the common core curriculum, it believed that instilling aesthetics as a mandatory course would give the subject the same level of respect as other requirements, namely the sciences and math.

The economic benefits of students advancing their studies in the sciences and math convinced the ministry that students would *not* invest in aesthetic studies without the subject being a requirement. Quoting the comments of the Committee of Inquiry into the Teaching of Art, Music and Dance, Bandara states, "Today we notice the regrettable situation that the most intelligent students in the schools choose science subjects, and have therefore no opportunity even if they are interested and talented, to pursue their studies in a fine art subject." Bandara praises the aesthetics education requirement as eliminating this discrepancy by allowing all students to access and learn the arts, irrespective of their major subject (1972, 37). For Bandara the learning of the arts must be an opportunity given to all. He couches the required subject as a choice—although it's clear that the range of choices available is limited. The formal syllabus and the potential to take exams in the subject ascribe importance to learning dance to the level of exams as an economic benefit. Aesthetics studies prepares students as future aesthetics teachers.

While teachers spoke of their many frustrations in teaching aesthetics in the government schools, the reality is that teaching in the schools is a stable and economically satisfying profession in an economy that has spent an exorbitant amount of its wealth on the war and financing defense. Bharata natyam certification allows students to obtain positions to continue their study in dance universities abroad, especially at Kalakshetra, the premier institution to learn Kalakshetra bharata natyam. Many teachers, including Sonia and another local teacher, Devini, studied dance in Colombo and then earned degrees in bharata natyam in India, returning with diplomas in dance that qualified them to teach in government schools. Reed states, "The only viable profession for a dancer in Sri Lanka is as a dance teacher" (2010, 145). Teaching is especially attractive to women dancers. It is a career with regular pay and hours that allow young women to travel between home and workplace during the daylight hours. It allows them to take up other supplemental teaching positions, as in the case of Sonia and Devini, who teach at arts organizations or their homes in the afternoons and weekends. It is a career that they can continue throughout their lives that allows them the flexibility demanded culturally—to have families, raise children—yet maintain economic and social independence, like Ganesan and the many other bharata natyam dance teachers in Colombo. As Kannagasabaratnam associated young girls with dance, this was the obvious trend. The teaching of bharata natyam through the aesthetics subject seems to imply that the female dancing body and the dance practice are inherently interconnected. In my research I did not learn of any male students learning bharata natyam in their school. The majority of, if not all, dance students were young girls.

In the aesthetics class bharata natyam is considered a classical dance tradition from India. As I discussed in the previous chapter, these distinctions of Indian, Tamil, or indigenous have political implications. When bharata natyam is classified as an Indian dance and is taught with more frequency in Tamil-medium schools, Tamils are associated with a larger Indian state and its culture and peoples.[14] Bharata natyam is ambivalently positioned to be part of the fabric of Colombo, yet outside the nation-state, the theory of the dance and the ways in which it is unevenly taught, along with the unevenness of the availability of Kandyan dance, can find a way to exclude Tamil bodies even more from belonging. Reed (2010) states that Tamil communities thought of bharata natyam and Tamil culture as superior to Kandyan and Sinhala forms, but, as a mandated curriculum of the state, it appears to be a partial offering. The curriculum of aesthetics can hide the shared experiences of Sinhala and Tamil bharata natyam dancers from history and from present understanding. And its inclusion and citation reflect a diversity that masks an unevenness in meaning, significance, and availability.

Sanchari Bhava #4: Pallika

After initially meeting at the college, Pallika invited me to tea at her home. Tucked away in a corner of a narrow street in the Borella neighborhood was her small, modest house. Her living room, furnished with only a few chairs and stools, served as her dance studio as well. Brown linoleum covered the floors, and on the walls hung several pictures of her and her son. She is a single mother. Her young son was outside playing close by in the neighborhood.

As we talked about her relationship and experience with bharata natyam, Kala, another visiting lecturer in bharata natyam who teaches at the university and is originally from Jaffna, walked in. Kala was just dropping by to visit. She visits Pallika often since she learns kathak from her. Watching both of them speak about learning from and teaching each other, I thought of how their forms and their bodies are constructed as different and even opposing. We all sat together, and Kala spoke Sinhala, a language she acquired only recently. Pallika kept complimenting Kala's mastery of the language. By the end of the conversation, as we were discussing the issues of the university (there have been several periods where the university was shut down due to strikes, protests, and political issues), Pallika told me that she is not interested in the ethnic conflict and, with pride, said, "I have some Tamil in me, you know. My grandmother was Tamil." Pallika's body and her dance practice question the rigid definitions of ethnicity and indigeneity espoused through the policies of the government and the aesthetics requirement.

Complexities, Contradictions, and Partial Conclusions

The Sinhala students studying bharata natyam are potentially future teachers of the dance. I met a handful of Sinhala bharata natyam dance teachers in Colombo who had visions for unity and peace in the country that stemmed from their exposure to what they identified as a Tamil cultural form. While critiquing and unmaking the frames that create the aesthetics curriculum is a central theme of this discussion in the questioning of the outcomes and practices in comparison to the theories that support its implementation, the dance *is* a means of connection through training, demonstrated through the conversations produced throughout this text. The dance has provided me a means to enter varied communities of dance through its common embodied language and a common experience—a common curriculum in its varied places, time frames, and politics.

This commonality is structured through a shared global vocabulary. The dance training has given me experiences from which to speak that intersect and provide a comparative form in which my interviewees and I can situate ourselves, whether we agree or not agree on protocols. Dance allows me to enter a conversation that features a range of experiences with performance, repertoire, musicians, composers, and choreographers throughout Colombo. Although I am not a graduate of the aesthetics requirement, Kannagasabaratnam's desires for the program as a means of connection among students through dance is partially demonstrated through the conversations that I have been able to engage in. It has provided a means for meaningful friendships and discussions, but it also cannot guarantee criticality and introspection and an understanding of power differences, especially if the content from the curriculum is taken as a unitary truth. Although Kannagasabaratnam's goals of the requirement are not manifested clearly within the classroom, exposure to bharata natyam has led many Sinhala students to pursue learning bharata natyam privately, through individual teachers and sometime organizations.

One teacher that benefits from this exposure is Ganesan, the Tamil teacher with whom I spoke. Her student base is diverse in terms of ethnicity and religious background, and several of her students started their bharata natyam studies in aesthetics. Her shared classrooms undo, momentarily, the types of segregation common in the institutional life of schooling and the arts (as demonstrated through the criticisms arising in her participation in the government program) and in neighborhoods, work environments, and arts spaces. She continues to create bharata natyam works that incorporate the backgrounds of her students, including various outside music and dance references.

Yet, in spite of this, Ganesan pointed out perceived and experienced differences in the ways in which people are respected and treated by the government based on geography and their position in the community, such as being an urban Colombo teacher as opposed to a Tamil teacher from the north or east. She benefits as a teacher from the assumed closeness with the government and her familiarity as a Colombo teacher. Her geographic base and her diverse student base allows her even more opportunities in these exclusive national stages, which restrict not only artists but wider publics. Dance practice carries a sense of safety and belonging—bharata natyam is included within the curriculum and within a state-sponsored performance, yet the everyday person is excluded from participating. Bharata natyam is included in the curriculum, but cultural nationalism precludes it from being considered a national form; it is instead considered foreign.

Aihwa Ong cites China as "deviant" in scholarship on neoliberalism because of how the country combines "neoliberal policies with state authoritarianisms" (2007, 4). Public education in Sri Lanka combines a developmental nationalism for equality and access through state governance. Yet the state was also tied to neoliberal policies supported by structural adjustment programs and foreign economic aid–intervention in the country. Greater growth encouraged technical and job-oriented curricula to become productive, self-sustaining, and cost-effective. Certifications, the marker of "diploma disease" (Engquist, Jivén, and Nyström 1981, 17), become an individually sought opportunity, injecting a measure of hopeful equal opportunity in a highly discriminate society, stratified by class, caste, and ethnic difference. Certifications are another means for class-oriented biases to continue—to provide justification for achievement or failure in a state of little economic growth. Yet test taking and certification-oriented curriculum has diminished creativity and critical thinking in the aesthetic curriculum.

Lisa Duggan proposed that one of the five phases of U.S. neoliberalism is an "emergent 'multicultural,' neoliberal 'equality politics'—a stripped-down, non-redistributive form of equality designed for global consumption during the twenty-first century, and compatible with continued upward redistribution of resources" (2003, xii). The aesthetics curriculum demonstrates state multiculturalism, unevenly distributed and limited in its economic scope toward the community and rigid through a cultural nationalism that restrains cultural practices. The abstracted form in theory and practice becomes more and more rooted in written knowledge, a denial of the historical malleability of the form, and its continuous engagement with the structures in which it finds itself. The form, one imbued with dispossession from traditional dance-and-drummer communities, requires an upward redistribution toward middle- and upper-class and caste students, who then seek employment by the state as a stable employer. The inclusion of dance in the state curriculum furthers the process of the dispossession that took place in the revival and recontexualization. Contemporary forms deny their use by the state through required state-sanctioned histories. Dancers then become part of state programs utilized to demonstrate cultural nationalism—the greatness of the state—and multiculturalism, the benevolence of the state to recognize minority cultures. The abstraction of the form returns bharata natyam to its position as an Indian dance that is a marker of Tamilness. It undoes the ethnic plurality that was engaged with the form. Its consideration as Indian, yet a marker of Tamilness, projects onto the Tamil body a sense of foreignness and a sense of gratefulness for its inclusion and representation within state employment.

The public education system in Sri Lanka has been the site of negotiating antineoliberal struggle. As discussed, it was a state institution that could visibly respond to the critiques of its own neoliberalism, where insurgencies demanded labor rights, local industry, and antidiscrimination policies. Yet it is an institution that has suffered greatly from state divestment. From 2.6 percent GDP allocation to education in 1954 to a maximum of 4.6 percent in 1964 (Kadirgamar 2015, 140), the proportion then decreased gradually due to the prioritizing of other means of developmental nationalism, cultural nationalism, and militarization. As of 2015, it was 1.8 percent of the GDP (139).

Women's bodies are the predominant site of aesthetic education in terms of both receiving (as students) and giving (as teachers). The practice sets the stage of women as embodiments of cultural nationalism, reproducing rigid forms and a disciplining of bodies for the national project. Their own bodies become markers of benevolence through their employment and their tales of success and incorporation. They train their bodies to incorporate such rigidity and find themselves stifled from innovation and from their own voice within their dance forms and from even speaking openly about their employers. Their bodies become the markers that can delegitimize community protest. Yet in their personal spaces, and even in their discreet and stifled criticisms, their experiences are acknowledged and their reluctant acceptance as a resounding and resolute critique.

3

Staging War
Choreographic Strategies during War

With the nubby carpeting and windowless walls, the room is similar to some of the classrooms in which I would find myself teaching in Canada a decade later, but it is Colombo. I turn the CD player on and place myself at the front, facing the rows of chairs that face me. With the music my feet move in a choreography of the imagined and envisioned dancing Ganesha, and using *nritya* I interpret the lyrics through gesture, body movements, and steps to describe the elephant-headed god with a protruding belly who holds in his hand *modakam*, his favorite sweet, whose feet move quickly—the beautiful dancing Ganesha: *Ananda Nardana Ganapati*.[1] Having performed these movements multiple times in the United States and Canada, I dance with little hesitation in this meeting room in the Fulbright complex in Colombo.[2] But the music stops suddenly, and I find myself halting midmove in this audition for the Fulbright organization's concert. The producers, Naveen and Asha, partners renowned for their musical and literary talents, respectively, respectfully ask me to sit. I take a seat in the second row, surprised at the brevity of my presentation, having prepared for this moment with hours of rehearsal in my apartment living room.

Kiran gets up from the first row and introduces himself by citing his training in Kandyan dance and yoga. He has brought a CD, *Incredible India*, and selects a melodic tune with numerous instruments, including the recognizable drone of the tambura that sets the pitch. His selected song, too, describes qualities of Ganesha, but through the commonly known shloka, "Vakratunda Mahakaya."[3] Kiran's dance is graceful, mirroring through the body the melody of the track. His moves are not lyrical interpretations of the shloka or *nritya* as emphasized in *Ananada Nardana Ganapati*. After a minute or two of slow movements, he stops himself and stands before the room to explain that this is the type of choreographic exploration he wishes to bring to the concert.

Turning to look at me, Asha asks, "Do you dance *only* to Carnatic music?" and adds that "Naveen will be composing the music, and it will be experimental." I quickly affirm that I can dance to anything, surprised by the question after the vigor and hustle of the dancing Ganesha that I attempted to portray in my piece. "You and Kiran should create a piece together," Naveen proposes. Kiran then suggests that he and I create a piece that stages "unity" and "hope" by bringing the two dance styles in which we're trained, Kandyan and bharata natyam, together. In efforts to also propose an idea, I add what I think to be a parallel theme insinuated by this discussion: war. But when my suggestion goes unacknowledged, I wonder if I have disturbed the proposal for peace through an acknowledgment of violence and if I have made myself the Other. I question whether my body as a foreign Tamil collapsed through an appropriation of an assumed monolithic Tamil body, "where the identity I had known in another context simply collapsed," as Dorinne Kondo articulates in her own ethnographic work (1990, 16). In this moment of voicing my thoughts, my inner voice amid my participation isn't benign; I knew I was implying a critique of the ongoing violence taking place around me and with it the patrolling of Tamilness in Colombo. My self-awareness and self-identification, as diasporic Tamil and bharata natyam dancer, seem too implicated in the politics of the country and the dance. But research demands my continued involvement, and I cannot exit the process.[4]

Kiran withdrew from the program because of demands on his schedule, so the collaboration never materialized, but the exchange highlights the intersections between dance choreography and the contemporary conditions of conflict. When Asha asked at the audition if I can dance *only* to Carnatic music, her question alludes to a common representation and imaginary of the bharata natyam dancer as limited in creativity and ultimately bounded by an unchanging, archaic form (this is further perpetuated through the education system, as discussed in the previous chapter). It highlights the ways in which bharata natyam dance is understood as tradition. The interaction between all of us during the audition urges a consideration of identity and choreography, subjectivity and dance, and asks how bodies shape dance productions. In the last chapter I discussed briefly how bodies and places resonate with suspicion or trust—through the choreographer and teacher Ganesan's perceived alliance with the government and the respect she was afforded as a local teacher from Colombo. This chapter furthers this discussion, primarily through explorations of choreography and place in Colombo. I ask, What are the underlying barriers and strategies employed to create pieces of contemporary relevance during an ongoing civil war? How do bodies—as producers of dance movement and markers of ethnicity—shape and impact contemporary choreographies?

To consider these questions I discuss two choreographic pieces staged in 2007 and explore how one choreographer purposefully employs choreographic tactics to address the war in the public arena. These performances were unique in the context of the war, when critiques and discourse concerning the conflict were limited to the leadership of the warring parties—whose war-ridden rhetoric assured safety among specific masses—and to leaders of organizations, journalists, and public intellectuals, whose work was to mobilize the people against militarization at great risk to themselves and their communities. Critiques by laypeople were often restricted to private spaces because of self- and state-surveillance that formed alongside the perpetuation of the war.

War associates bodies and certain geographies with safety or danger. With its progression a cartography of safe and unsafe neighborhoods is produced, distinguished by symbols, bodies, associated histories, and contemporary ideologies. Pradeep Jeganathan (2003) insightfully draws on how Colombo is an ever-shifting terrain of "anticipatory violence" of places attacked or attractive to attack. Homes, neighborhoods, and roads are material intersections of past memory and contemporary circumstance. They locate past trauma and loss and exist in the unpredictable undulation of the present—inexorably influenced by current-day politics of war. In her anthropology of the war in Sri Lanka in displaced communities inside and outside of Colombo, Sharika Thiranagama states, "The city offers itself constantly as a space of life and death simultaneously, its sounds and sights to be read with anxious gaze and speculative ear" (2011, 244).

Continuing in the vein of Jeganathan's (2003) site-specific analysis of Colombo and following the spatial theorizations of Henri Lefebvre, I am interested in how (social) space evokes a (social) reality (1991, 26). Lefebvre poses several questions in the introduction of *The Production of Space*:

> Is this space an abstract one? Yes, but it is also "real" in the sense in which concrete abstractions such as commodities and money are real. Is it then concrete? Yes, though not in the sense that an object or product is concrete. Is it instrumental? Undoubtedly, but, like knowledge, it extends beyond instrumentality. Can it be reduced to a projection—to an "objectification" of knowledge? Yes and no: knowledge objectified in a product is no longer coextensive with knowledge in its theoretical state. If space embodies social relationships, how and why does it do so? And what relationships are they? (26–27)

Lefebvre's space is dynamic, processual, and influential. The geography of war and conflict is similar, though it pursues control through naming and predetermining space and lives by way of ideological thinking and declarations of secure and dangerous, and ally and enemy, to unmake and make people and place through the abstract—war's rhetoric—and the real: militarization and security. Here bharata natyam, deploys its (social) choreography according to the (social) space in which it's performed. Choreography based on the "archive" and those formed through new "repertoire" (concepts discussed by D. Taylor [2003]) are employed strategically to navigate time and place. Onto those bodies that compose the audience, the choreographer—and the ethnographer—project ideological representations and significances. Dance is strategically embodied, performed, *and* even written about, through the process of being "made" and "unmade" through war. As Sharika Thiranagama states, "the war 'happened' 'to' people and at the same time made them" (2011, 10). In her evocative anthropology of those displaced by war, she discusses "wartime selves" created through war's mechanisms (11). As much as worlds of family, home, caste, and tradition are destroyed by the upheaval of war, such experiences are also productive through the shaping of subjectivity. For instance, a daughter raised with the experience of war, where repressive militarization was pervasive to a point of "normal," was made differently from her mother, who experienced a youth not marked with militarization and who would experience motherhood with a child unable to experience the freedom associated with youth and education (48).

In the time and space of the Fulbright audition, where I was a foreign researcher and an invited performer, I was able to voice a suggestion in my attempt at inclusion and critique, only to be faced with a feeling of miscomprehension and failure. It is this sense of reflexivity, cynicism, and desire on the part of the researcher that shapes the process of writing this chapter.[5] Offering doubt is not to retract the assertions made by the close reading of choreography or this larger study but to expose tensions of war and dance alongside the ethnographer's continuously emerging subjectivity in writing and living in Colombo during the war.

Draupadhi Sabatham

The signifier, we recall, cannot be detached from the
individual or collective body.
—D. Taylor (2003, 8)

On a Saturday in May 2007, I attended the seventy-fifth anniversary celebration of the Tamil Maanavar Sangam, or Tamil Students Union of the Ladies' College, in Cinnamon Gardens, a posh neighborhood of Colombo. Outside the school gates was a well-dressed crowd, excited about the presentation, just minutes away. Walking past young women in their matching saris of pastel chiffons, I entered the rustic auditorium and took a seat.

Those same young women I passed at the entrance would gather onstage shortly to open the event. Standing on risers, they assembled to sing, "Tamizh Mozhi Vaazhttu" (translated loosely as "In praise of the Tamil language"). The song is a composition of Subramania Bharati (1882–1921), a Tamil poet from Tamil Nadu, India. He was an Indian independence fighter, social reformer who argued for the rights of women, and devotee to the Goddess. An iconic lover of the Tamil language, literature, and its people, Mahakavi Bharathiyar (the Great Poet Bharati, as he was known) composed several songs and poems that praised the greatness of Tamil, a well-known example of which is, "Tamizh Mozhi Vaazhttu."

> Long live the living and enduring Tamil language, long live!
> Taking within it the sky and myself, long live colorful Tamil!
> Long live the music holding my heart, which is held by the seven seas!
> Long live Tamil, long live Tamil! (Bharati 1990, 46; translation mine)

It was not the first time that I had heard Bharati's works in Colombo. In fact, I had come across his work quite frequently. His famous poem, "Kaani Nilam Vendum" (translated loosely as I need a piece of land) often aired between television programs on the Tamil-language television channel, Shakthi TV:

> A piece of land I crave, Goddess Great!
> A piece of land I crave:
> A pillared beauty hall
> Where variegated hues enthrall;
> In heart of that fair land
> A palace you must build

A well to quench my thirst

And coconut leaves to burst (Bharati 1979, 19)

Upon seeing this concise "public service announcement" message that traced the Tamil words under a sketch of Bharati's face, I was surprised that such a political request, inherently asking for land—a central motive of the Tamil Tigers separatist struggle—was broadcast into people's homes with such frequency. I inquired about its relevance to the conflict in Sri Lanka. My friends admitted that Sri Lanka's war had not crossed their minds. Such interactions made me wonder if I am too conscious of the war and whether such consciousness demonstrated a lack of immersion in Colombo and Sri Lanka. For me the war was not mundane and would never be. Yet, for most around me, its seeming perpetuity and reoccurrence made it just that. The regularity of the invocation of Bharati on the television and his canonization into the field of Tamil literature—inscribed into a literary Tamil tradition—appeared to depoliticize the requests innate in his writing, transforming his political stance into an apolitical routine and severing his anticolonial and nationalist politics from the contemporary nationalist and separatist conflict in Sri Lanka.[6]

However, his play *Panchali Sabatham* (Draupadhi's curse) in the dance-theater performance of *Draupadhi Sabatham* was chosen to address the contemporary circumstance of war intensifying around us.[7] *Draupadhi Sabatham* drew from Bharati's edited scene from the *Mahabharata*, a Sanskrit epic.[8] The epic tells the tale of two sets of cousins (the Pandavas and Kauravas), who were raised, trained, and educated together but would eventually fight a deadly war against each other, killing family and teachers (gurus). The five Pandava princes are the protagonists throughout the epic, as the hundred-brother Kaurava clan continually vies for power against them. Draupadhi is the wife of all five Pandava princes.

In Tamil and English the voice-over introduced *Draupadhi Sabatham* as "a scene from the epic the *Mahabharata*," an epic that displayed the consequences of depraved "jealousy between cousins, causing a war within the family." Did the audience, like me, reflect on the war in Sri Lanka upon hearing the words, "war within the family"?[9] Was the word "war" heard so frequently that it has lost its meaning and emotional impact, just like Bharati-yar's "Kaani Nilum Vendum"?

Draupadhi Sabatham began with Duryodhana of the Kaurava clan on-stage. Danced by an all-girls troupe dressed as princes, the dancers were bejeweled with golden crowns and hefty black beards and moustaches. Set on destroying the prosperity of his cousins—the Pandavas—Duryodhana approached his uncle Shakuni, who, as described in the lyrics, is "an embodiment of lies and cunningness."[10] The stances of the two men were wide, and their elbows were positioned away from their torso, while their hands were held in fists, true to their roles as scheming royal figures. With their arms shifting from folded at the chest to holding the chin, they strutted back and forth, conjuring a scheme to cheat Yudishthira, the eldest brother and leader of the Pandavas, out of his kingdom. "Let me know a way to destroy the five brothers and Draupadhi," gestured Duryodhana along with the sung lyrics. The "evil-hearted uncle" Shakuni devised a plan for the Kaurava clan to win over the Pandava Kingdom. Expressing with "slimy words" and quick, successive mudras (hand gestures), he suggested that Duryodhana and the Kauravas invite the Pandava princes over to play a game of dice. He revealed to Duryodhana that the game would be rigged so that Duryodhana will always win. As he looked from side to side slyly, Uncle Shakuni clasped his hands. Duryodhana wondered whether Uncle Shakuni's plan would work, his eyebrows knitted as he pondered the idea. Finally, he agreed, nodding.

Yudishthira succumbed to the Kauravas' scheme in the second and final scene. He wagered the wealth, army, and kingdom of the Pandavas, then his brothers and himself and, finally, Draupadhi. She was the final wager. Sung lyrics in Tamil mark the defeat:

He lost himself
Aiyo! Aiyo! Draupadhi—
In the gamble is lost
Aiyo! (Kulendran 2007; translation mine)

With their final win the conniving Kauravas were ready to collect their prize. "Bring her, oh brother, bring her. . . . She, whose beautiful eyes are dark like the rain clouds. Today onward, she is mine!" Duryodhana commanded, facing the wings. Dushasana, the younger brother of Duryodhana and dressed similarly, entered the stage. With him was Draupadhi, portrayed by a tall thin dancer in a blue-and-white sari costume, whom he dragged by her long black hair with tight fists or *mushti* mudras.[11] Draupadhi grabbed the side of her head in pain; her eyes were worried, and her body winced away from her attacker. Dushasana pushed her to the ground with open hands, gesturing with *pataka* mudras.[12] The Pandava brothers looked with shame at the scene before them but remained still, helpless in their new condition as property of their cousins.

With her mouth open in shock and her hands extended away shielding her as she was chased in circles on the stage's periphery, Draupadhi was silently screaming. Fallen before the men of the court, she appeared shocked at her circumstances, her eyes large and confused. She finally lifted herself to notice the presence of her husbands; her gaze stopping at each and every one of them but left unreturned. Shakuni ordered her to be stripped, and Dushasana lunged toward her with a *mushti* mudra to suggest the pulling of her sari. With the sari's unraveling Draupadhi started to spin. After a set of spins, Draupadhi faced the audience and called out, asking for divine inter-vention. Lord Krishna granted her a sari of infinite length, performed for the audience through her seemingly endless spins. Krishna, unseen, pro-vided Draupadhi's rescue as a bell rang in the musical accompaniment.

Facing the audience, Draupadhi's anger surfaced. She stated her vow, which echoed the vow in Bharati's 1912 *Panchali Sabatham* to the Goddess Parashakti:

> In Parashakti's name I take this vow:
> Not till the fiend Dushasana's red blood
> Mingles with demon Duryodhana's,
> And I smear my tresses with their blood
> And then bathe and wash it all away—
> Not till then will I gather again
> These my tresses unloosened and wild! (Bharati 1977)

Upon this utterance, Draupadhi, her eyes large and her hands stiff with rage, was lit with a center spotlight and surrounded by the Pandavas, who stared at their cousins with equal conviction. The syllable of "om" sounded three times, as if to seal the vow.[13] The faces of the Kauravas showed worry and fear. The lights went to black.

The audience was silent for a moment until applause set in. They soon began to converse with one another and gather their items to leave the audi-torium. But questions filled my mind as I sat looking toward the stage. Who did Draupadhi represent? Was this representation tied to the players in the local conflict? Who onstage represented the government? The Tigers? The people of Sri Lanka? Did Draupadhi symbolize the civilian wagered in a game played by the LTTE and the government? In this performance all char-acters, aside from Draupadhi, were culpable as witnesses to the wager. Various possible combinations and connections flooded my thoughts. What I did know was that the choreographer, Chandran, wanted to present a piece on war for the Tamil Students Union of the Ladies' College. She commissioned a local Tamil scholar, singer, and composer, Kulendran, to write not only the music for the entire drama but the lyrics as well.

The connection to the contemporary moment and the local context was not expressed overtly in *Draupadhi Sabatham*. The story is part of what Diana Taylor names "the archive." The archive consists of material pieces such as documents, maps, literary texts, videos, and archaeological remains that are "supposedly resistant to change" (2003, 19). A story like the *Mahabharata* is a corpus that is recalled, often in parts, in several dance practices from South Asia, such as *kathakali* to Southeast Asia and the Wayang Kulit puppetry of Java ("On Versions" 2004). Like *Antigone*, the epic Taylor recalls in her analysis of the archive and the repertoire, the *Mahabharata* "might be performed in multiple ways, while the unchanging texts assures a stable signifier" and "what changes over time is the value, relevance or meaning of the archive, how the items it contains get interpreted, even embodied" (2003, 11). The *Mahabharata* and its excerpt of the attempted rape of Draupadhi is a story globally staged. The U.S.-based bharata natyam dance company in which I performed included this excerpt in its popular touring production for almost ten years. In that instance the excerpt was included in a larger production on divine powers and the faults of humanity. The story of the attempted rape was featured as an example of greed, and the choreography brought particular attention to Yudishthira's folly. When I spoke to the composer commissioned to write the Carnatic score, Kulendran, she emphasized that Chandran chose the performance to bring the topic of the war to the stage.

There were several metaphoric parallels with Sri Lanka's war: for one, the voice-over, "war within the family," introduced *Draupadhi Sabatham*. The portrayal of the Kauravas and Pandavas, first cousins who engage in a great battle that results in the death of many—family, friends, and citizens—resonated with the Sri Lankan context. The danced drama mirrored the civil conflict that dismisses shared families, histories, beliefs, and practices between Sinhala and Tamils to create distinct factions as contemporary ethnicities. Second, competition as the precursor to war succinctly paralleled the country's civil conflict and the consequential violence rooted in episodic political maneuvers for power. Like the Pandavas and Kauravas, political groups and official and unofficial parties were proven complicit to, if not leading the perpetuation of, violence toward "non-participants" and innocent citizens (Tambiah 1986, 13; Little 1994, 4–7). Third, the attack on Draupadhi highlighted the suffering of civil society. Both the Kauravas and the Pandavas appeared to be one and the same as they wagered for possession of the noncombatant in their larger game of dice. Fourth, Draupadhi, as the only woman in the work (and the only one physically violated) was significant. Her body was the prize for the highest wager in the game between the family members. Sexual violence against women is a device of war. As Kanchana Ruwanpura states, women's bodies have become "the primary site for declaring the power of one ethnic group over another" (2008, 104).[14] Chandran's selection of *Draupadhi Sabatham* was certainly a compelling parable that visualized an encounter of assault often made invisible in narratives of war. Finally, Draupadhi's concluding call for vengeance emulated the cycle of retaliatory violence that pervaded the twenty-six-year war.

Draupadhi Sabatham appeared to subversively insert a reflection on the war through its use of the archive. The tale of Draupadhi's attempted rape is widely familiar in its basic form. It is retold through its frequent recollection in bharata natyam performance with a sense of deference similar to the recitation of Bharati's works as part of the Tamil literary canon. The format of the piece *Draupadhi Sabatham* was in the dance-drama style made popular through the Kalakshetra bharata natyam. The revival of bharata natyam dance, and the use of dance dramas in the repertoire, broke with known devadasi "traditions" but became acceptable in the revived dance practice (Allen 1997). Having performed the same scene in a Chicago-based dance company for years, I saw that the number of characters, the sequence of the events within the story, the format of interpretation of the sung words of the characters alongside a sung narration of events through *nritya* and abhinaya were common to my own experience learning and performing. Drawing on the movement and choreographic components of bharata natyam common to dance-drama productions, *Draupadhi Sabatham* was also contemporary and singular as a premier production with a newly composed Carnatic score.

The use of this archive, set in this Tamil event, was seen as following tradition—and it was—specifically with practices formed as repertoire in the bharata natyam revival. Chandran's astute adherence to tenets of Kalakshetra style was perceived as an adherence to the classical and to Tamil language and culture, such that the production could be included in the seventy-fifth anniversary festivities of the Tamil Students Union. Tamil bodies, language, and culture were prominent at this celebration of the organization. Bharati's "Tamizh Mozhi Vaazhttu," sung at the beginning, is an exposition of deep love for the Tamil language. *Panchali Sabatham* in its iteration by Bharati resonated with political significance. Bharati utilized the rape of Panchali (Draupadhi) as a metaphor for the British colonization of India, where Panchali was a symbol of "Mother India" (Hiltebeitel 1981).

Yet at this arena of the seventy-fifth anniversary of the Tamil Maanavar Sangam, the complexity of the Sri Lankan conflict that surrounded us did not permit easy and clear connections in the narrative; such connections needed to be discreetly derived. The public service announcement of Bharati's "Kanni Nilum Vendum" on the television, which entered between scheduled programs, and its insertion in-between events on screen in the everyday relegated it to inconsequential and unrelated to the contemporary moment and politics. The deployment of the literary icon's work at the seventy-fifth anniversary concert fit the mundane, regular occurrence of the recital of "classical" Tamil culture. Bharati (a literary figure) and bharata natyam (an embodied practice) are deployed often in Tamil spaces and viewed as vestiges of Tamil culture—as traditional (spiritual and devotional) practices distinct from the baseness of contemporary politics. Bharati (as a Tamil icon) and bharata natyam (as Tamil practice) inspired little introspection or investigation as notion of tradition, of the classical; they were seemingly self-contained tools of preservation and survival not subject to change and influence. The dance form's status as traditional and classical, amplified through its textual base (through the *Natya Shastra*) emphasized and constructed during the dance form's revival, renders it fixed and timeless, as works of the archive are often perceived. Thus, when Asha asks me, "Do you dance *only* to Carnatic music?" she is asking a question based on a perception of the classically oriented bharata natyam dancer that sees such training as "limited" to a rigid and spiritual tradition. The archive—the tradition—is perceived and also practiced as separated from the local and temporal context, from a sense of creative presence, dynamism, and interpretation.

The "repertoire," according to Diana Taylor, is unlike the archive in its ephemerality and embodied quality through its requirement of presence of people to be part of the transmission. It can "keep" as it "transforms choreographies of meaning" (2003, 20). In bharata natyam repertoire is shaped through the period of the form's revival and its negotiations between embodied practices and textual sources such that even the most traditional choreography is not completely fixed: it transforms in the process of its transmission. A conventional bharata natyam piece consists of a compilation of phrases set to the music of a dance style customary repertoire. Dance teachers arrange material learned from their mentors but assembled according to their own decisions. (O'Shea 2007, 27)

The utilization of a canonical story for the anniversary participated in maintaining the event's traditions. The use of the dance-drama format, read as part of bharata natyam tradition, allowed Chandran to avoid criticism from many bharata natyam practitioners and audience members. Some Colombo-based practitioners believe that bharata natyam should not portray themes outside of Hindu texts and Carnatic repertoires or use choreographic formats outside of margam repertoire or the accepted dance-drama form. One particular teacher, Yogendran, who trained in Jaffna under Ramiah Pillai, said,

Someone asked me, "Why don't you do more social themes?" I said that "There is drama for social themes." In dance, there are more religious themes, so that's what we do. There are compositions by Alvars, Aandaal, so we do that. Then the people who come [and see the dance] want to learn what the religion is. If all of us turn to social themes and contemporary dancing, they won't know what bharata natyam is and what the religious aspect is.[15]

For Yogendran bharata natyam dance practice must adhere to religious practice. To emphasize her point, Yogendran recalls renowned Tamil Hindu saints who wrote religious literature as source material for bharata natyam choreography.

But the production, through this accepted and commonly understood traditional form, allowed for a critical insertion at a moment of expanding militarization of the city. It permitted the dance to be perceived as mundane and apolitical but incorporated with it a commentary on the local context of war. For the ethnographer—a dancer and spectator—war hardly blurred into the ordinary. Instead, the war and the dance practice in it were extraordinary. Performing the dice game in both the United States and in India in the past didn't make *Draupadhi Sabatham* expected to the ethnographer. Instead, it was an unconventional and strategic performance in Colombo taking place in the 2007 as militarization developed further throughout the city, demarcating spaces and people as secure and dangerous.

The largely Tamil gathering of the seventy-fifth anniversary of the Tamil Students Union can be considered a "soft" target for violence (Jeganathan 2003). The state, which was rooting out Tamils from the city and subjecting Tamil residents to random searches, could justifiably police such gatherings. In a later report Keheliya Rambukwella, a government minister and the spokesperson for the Ministry of Defense, "acknowledged Tamils were singled out for scrutiny in Colombo, but only because rebel attackers—who have killed members of all ethnic groups—routinely hid among the capital's large Tamil community" (Nessman 2008). It meant that any Tamil gathering or space was subject to suspicion. The dynamics of this patrolled geography were intricate. Wealthier parts of the city were under military security, increasing their potential as targets of the Tigers' attacks, whereas poorer and working-class Tamil neighborhoods were scrutinized as hosting Tigers in their midst. Venues located in Tamil neighborhoods appeared more open to being the setting for performances, but since they were increasingly subject to surveillance, they were not seen as suitable settings for the performances. At the time of the two performances discussed here, the city had closed parking lots to performance venues and street parking was no longer permitted in certain areas of the city.

The familiar format of dance drama and the often-excerpted *Mahabharata* in bharata natyam repertoire allowed Chandran to stage a piece on the war that implicitly referenced the contemporary conflict, lessening the suspicion believed to be cast on the bodies in this space. Like the Pandavas and Kauravas, political groups and official and unofficial parties have been complicit in initiating episodes of violence and perpetuating the devastation of "non-participants" or innocent citizens (Little 1994, 4–7; Tambiah 1986, 13). In its portrayal of the victimization of Draupadhi, *Draupadhi Sabatham* highlighted the suffering of civil society. Watching the performance, I was reminded of the citizens in Colombo (and elsewhere on the island) who in 2007 endured daily checks at security checkpoints, early morning raids of homes and personal property, and the "white van syndrome," where a mysterious unmarked van abducted people off the streets, leading to a growing number of disappearances.

Draupadhi, as the only female in the work and the only person physically violated, is significant. Her body is the prize for the highest wager in

Newspaper ad by the National Anti War Front. Photo by the author.

the game between the family members—land is often feminized, ideologically, with war. And, with war, the violation of women's bodies has been a constant. The use of women's bodies as a means of one ethnic group asserting power over another "exacerbates violence against women from the same community" (Ruwanpura 2008, 104). Draupadhi's concluding cry for vengeance mirrored the narratives of the violation of women's bodies used to embolden the conflict and further divisions. Neloufer De Mel states in *Women and the Nation's Narrative: Gender and Nationalism in Twentieth Century Sri Lanka*:

> The fate of beauty queen Premawathie Manamperi, who was raped and killed by the army in 1971, continued to dominate JVP discourse in a highly sexualized manner for it was her violated body that was remembered and recovered in JVP songs, posters and articles that appeared in the JVP newspaper *Niyamuwa*. Manamperi became a mnemonic by which to recall state terror. The JVP discourse of her rape and death was used to transfer the responsibility for acts of violence solely onto the state and to project the JVP as the victim, not perpetrators, of violence in its own right. When Dhanu killed Ragiv Gandhi, the LTTE put out a message that the Indian Peace Keeping Force (IPKF) had raped her and that her act of violence was a fitting revenge for her shame and trauma. It is significant that in both instances, rape was publicized only once the women were dead. As for the living female cadre, the sexual abuses they suffered remained silenced, censored. This silence may have allowed the JVP women to re-enter the social mainstream but it did nothing to redress the wrongs committed by the security forces to inaugurate a public discussion on women's bodies as sites of war. (2001, 220)[16]

De Mel (2001) speaks to the underlying subordination of women in the war, as civilians and militants, and discusses how women's bodies are utilized for political gain. Draupadhi is a figure that would also have to accept the decisions of her husbands' family: she was won through competition and instructed to accept the five brothers as her husband. The curse she pronounces at the end is one of the only times, I was taught, she would ever speak her wishes and demonstrate a sense of agency. Her declaration, however, was contingent on those to whom she was already dependent. Chandran's selection of the attempted rape of Draupadhi was certainly a compelling parable, especially in the setting of an all-girls' school. Draupadhi's concluding cry for vengeance mirrored the ongoing conflict in Sri Lanka as each political party engaged in a cycle of retaliation for previous transgressions. This call for vengeance performed before a largely Tamil audience may also be more than incidental, echoing the complex relationships between the Tamils and the LTTE. This relationship straddled both respect for the rebel army (for standing up to the discriminatory policies of the Sri Lankan government) and detestation of it (as its own authoritarian methods silenced any peace-loving Tamil and Sinhala voices), while controlling the Sri Lankan Tamil community both in Sri Lanka and in the diaspora. Finally, the performance mirrored the conflict where nationalism had created distinct conceptions of and histories for Tamils and Sinhala. To this day there are many shared histories, beliefs, practices, and even kinship between the Sinhala and the Tamils. This became the focus of the next choreography, *Shanti*.

Shanti

"This will be a unique opportunity for you," Chandran said on the phone, as she invited me to her students' arangetram, an evening-length debut performance. It would be unique because it was a joint arangetram for two of her students, Shankari (Tamil) and Anushka (Sinhala). Chandran was also presenting a new choreography created especially for the occasion. The arangetram was held in Bishop's College Auditorium in Cinnamon Gardens, Colombo 7. Chandran mentioned that it had become difficult to find spaces to hold arangetrams because of the war. Parking lots were now closed, and street parking in certain areas was no longer permitted. Cinnamon Gardens (the neighborhood that houses the residences of the president and prime minister, the University of Colombo, high-end shopping areas, and beautiful, sprawling mansions) was an area especially affected by the new regulations.

On that day the closed parking lot of Bishop's College Auditorium required the slew of cars to pull up awkwardly to the venue, while audience members dressed in rich silks and security staff dressed in militarized uniforms tried to guide vehicles out quickly. Directions were yelled out to drivers, arranging for ways of meeting after the concert, knowing that the confusion now would be replicated again later. But in spite of the commotion, the lobby of Bishop's College Auditorium was filled with cheerful and mingling guests that Saturday evening. Two distinct groups of young girls, one Tamil and one Sinhala, welcomed guests. A few of the young Tamil women wore the conventional style of the sari, while some wore the *paavadai thavani* (half saris) with a long skirt (*paavadai*), blouse, and shawl tied around the waist and draped over the left shoulder. The Sinhala girls all wore the Kandyan-style sari (identified as traditional Sinhala-style, although from a few conversations I've had there are caste differences demonstrated in the various ways of tying of the sari).

The young Tamil women distributed some Hindu Tamil essentials: *cakrai* (rock sugar), *kumkum* (vermillion), and *candanam* (sandalwood paste). They also sprinkled rosewater from the *paniir chembu* on willing guests. Because of my responsibility to experience the event fully to write about it later, I was a more than willing guest and participated in all the services offered. I gladly accepted all these gifts, enjoying the slightly floral scent of the sandalwood, the cooling beads of water hitting my scalp and dripping through my hair, and the hard sweetness of sugar melting in my mouth. Willing to continue my experience of being formally welcomed, I walked over to the second group of young Sinhala women. They distributed *cakrai* mixed with dried and roasted lentils. Guests did not visit both groups as I did; instead, they paused at the entrance to take notice of the two groups and chose one from which to receive the gifts.

Upon seeing Chandran, I approached her. But before we could speak, she was asked to greet the chief guest of honor and left me instead holding her purse. "I'll be back," she said. I watched as she was introduced to the special guest by the parents of both girls. After the formalities Chandran walked back to me, collected her purse, and said, "I'm happy you could make it. It should be something special that you haven't seen before." I was happy and relieved to be so warmly welcomed by her. I was constantly nervous with socializing in this new-to-me city, where I didn't know many people. My singleness—singularity—made me noticeably different, without anyone to connect with. But once Chandran left to go backstage, I surprisingly found a few familiar faces among the crowd: dance students whom I had interviewed, a mother with whom I had spoken. After exhausting the list of familiar folks, I decided to go find a seat in the middle row on the right side, which allowed me to see the orchestra.

The program began with the master of ceremonies providing, in English, a brief history of bharata natyam, identifying it as an Indian dance form and connecting the dance to the *Natya Shastra*, subsequently tracing the dance's roots to the second century CE. This history made no reference to the practice as a reconstructed form. I had become familiar with this means of introduction and this popular history of bharata natyam, having heard it both in Chicago and Colombo—a succinct yet selective narrative that contextualized the form to an unfamiliar audience. Any introduction to the form was markedly absent from the *Tamil Maanavar Sangham*—the Tamil Students Union event at the Ladies' College—discussed earlier. There the dance was assumed familiar and part of Tamil culture. The history delivered at the arangetram placed the roots of the dance elsewhere, not spatially or temporally close, but far—in India and in the ancient past. It tied the form to a distinctly spiritual practice, yet there were clear differences between the time and space of these forms, for unlike the event that marks the beginning of the devadasi's inauguration into ritual and dance practices, the contemporary arangetram among the South Asian diaspora, and even in Sri Lanka, often marks the termination of dance study. Instead of being a lifetime commitment to ritual and artistic labor as it was for the devadasi, the contemporary arangetram in Sri Lanka fits with its global counterparts as an opportunity for both Tamil and Sinhala families to present their daughters to "their own community," marking "their respectability as women and daughters" through the demonstration of culture and arts (O'Shea 2007, 155). It is also an opportunity to display family wealth to the community. The multiplicity of contexts that preceded and converged with the revived form of bharata natyam dance were not part of the narrative onstage, nor of how these previous contexts took place on the island that would become Sri Lanka (Soneji 2010).

As my knowledge of the form cast judgment on the practices before me, others' opinions came to mind. When a Hindu priest took to the stage to perform a short *puja* for the Nataraja at stage right, the audience came to their feet for the ritual blessing of the dancers' ankle bells. I watched the priest light the lamp as an offering, and the words of a Colombo-based dance teacher trained primarily in Jaffna came to my mind: "When I was in Jaffna, we'd do the *puja* behind the curtain. Now it's in front of everyone. It's better to do it behind the curtain. It's a cosmopolitan crowd that comes [i.e., a mixed crowd of Sinhala and non-Hindus]; we don't have to make everyone stand up and do that."[17] Yogendran's comments expose the diversity of views and how one's tradition can challenge another's with a community. For her, multiculturalism's desire for performing shared beliefs can undo the exact difference it supposedly aims to preserve and protect. Although aspects of the arangetram such as contextualizing of the form, the *puja*, and the choreographies onstage were seen and rhetorically spoken of as tradition and unchanging, they were negotiated and understood differently by the bodies in space and place.

The opening of the curtain revealed the Carnatic musical accompaniment with a vocalist, *mridangist* (drummer), violinist, and Chandran on *nattuvangam* seated stage left—visible from my seat.[18] The first half of the program drew from items in the margam repertoire (*alarippu*, jatiswaram, *sabdam*, and *varnam*, the format standardized by the musician-composers of the Thanjavur Quartet in the nineteenth century), and each song was danced together, mostly in unison, to Tamil lyrics (O'Shea 2007, 26). The second half included shorter compositions labeled by the master of ceremonies as *padams*, but the pieces didn't feature the tripartite relationship signature to the *padam* genre, with a *nayaki* (a female devotee), a *nayaka* (a male deity or patron), and a *sakhi* (the mediator or friend) who carries the message of the devotee. Shankari's pieces were devotional songs that often praised various aspects of God or the Goddess and fit the genre of *kirtanams*, Carnatic compositions included in bharata natyam repertoires during the revival (Allen 1997). Anushka's pieces were in the Sinhala language, and instead of being accompanied by the Carnatic orchestra that played for all the dance pieces thus far, her solos were to taped music. Both of the dancers used mudras and abhinaya from bharata natyam to interpret the lyrics (*nritya*) and danced *nritta* during rhythmic breaks in the song. The second half of the program demonstrated how personal arangetrams have become—incorporating songs that are family favorites, demonstrating the students' religious and ethnic identities.

After the solo items that marked the second half of the program, the master of ceremonies announced that in lieu of the *mangalam* that customarily closes the dance performance, Anushka and Shankari would present a newly choreographed and composed piece, *Shanti* (Peace). But before dancing the final item, Anushka and Shankari took to the lectern and gave brief speeches, introducing themselves in each other's language, to which the audience clapped and cheered. Everyone appreciated this gesture.

As *Shanti* opened, the stage was aglow in a red wash. Sounds of gunshots and bombs flooded the auditorium as they were played on a synthesizer in the accompanying orchestra. The empty stage quickly filled with running bodies as Anushka and Shankari sprinted from opposite corners diagonally crossing to the other side. Expressing fear as they ran with their arms extended to provide shelter, they crossed the stage over and over again, not acknowledging each other's presence. Crouched on opposite sides, the fear on their faces shifted to worry and then sorrow. As the sounds of war faded and the red lights thinned to faint, with trepidation, the dancers slowly lifted their heads and noticed each other's presence across stage, their eyes finally meeting. Looking at each other, both slowly unfolded themselves and walked toward stage center. Suddenly, the red lights pulsed on and off, accompanied by the sounds of the bombs and gunshots. The dancers crouched again, this time covering each other with their arms. Moving their hands back and forth from their heads to their ears, they clutched each other as the sounds faced and the redness of the lights dissipated. As they raised themselves from their stooped positions, a prayer-song began. The lyrics of the music, alternating between Tamil and Sinhala, made a request for peace:

> We want peace to flourish everywhere—in the world
> We want peace to flourish everywhere
> Expansive and vast love—in the world
> We want peace to flourish everywhere. . . .
> Without jealousy, without hatred, without war
> By living peace will flourish—that
> In our hearts gives strength, honesty, and character
> Only one way will show—that's the reason
> Wickedness goes and goodness blooms—in the world.

Facing the audience, Anushka and Shankari used *nritya*, the synchronization of hand gestures and facial expressions (mudras and abhinaya) to enact the lyrics as they were repeated in Sinhala and Tamil. After several repetitions of the lyrics, *Shanti* concluded with recited invocations from Buddhist (*Buddham saranam gacchami, dhammam saranam gacchami, sangham saranam gacchami*) and Hindu (*Om shanti shanti shanti*) religious traditions.[19] The dancers faced the audience as each held their hands in *anjali* mudra, moving their hands in unison from above their heads to their foreheads and then to their hearts.[20]

This explicit reference to the war surprised me. The heightened militarization in Colombo imposed an eerie silence in public spaces, restraining open critique of the surroundings and their connected politics. Often when I walked in the city I was stopped, along with other pedestrians, as roads emptied of civilian vehicles so that ministerial vehicles, escorted by the army, could swiftly proceed. We stood, silent and motionless, as military vehicles passed by. Although billboards and military hardware referenced the conflict incessantly, people's discussions of the war were in intimate spaces.

In her anthropology of former militants and those displaced through the war, Thiranagama states,

> One common way of describing war by Tamils in Sri Lanka was to tell me of the fear they felt towards other Tamils, unsure of who was LTTE and who was not. "There is no trust (*nambikkai*) among Tamils any more" was a frequent phrase. LTTE's often forcible recruitment of ordinary Tamils from families, and its widespread intelligence network and seeming pervasive presence in the Tamil community had led to a situation where networks of trust among Tamils were shrinking. The battlefields of the war were not only the frontlines where LTTE cadres and Sri Lankan soldiers died, but were also the internal lives of Tamil communities and families. (2011, 10)

Distinctions existed between public and private, the feared and the trusted, outside one's home and within it. Yet these distinctions were not always clear. The complicated intermingling of the Tigers in the larger Tamil community (especially through methods of forced recruitment) created self-patrolling in these spaces. There was external patrolling of Tamil bodies by the state, made visible in Colombo with the numerous checkpoints throughout the city and at the borders of predominantly Tamil areas, the random searching of homes in Tamil neighborhoods, and the forced evacuation of Tamils from Colombo.

Shared experiences of war were the focus of *Shanti* and, through them, unity and hope the theme. The piece may have fit the vision of Asha and Naveen at the Fulbright audition. *Shanti* made visible a sense of terror across divisions of identity and boundaries of geography. Yet the movements in the choreography were similar to the images caught on mobile phones of Tamil civilians caught in the shelling during the final war: taking shelter, running from place to place, and falling into small trenches as bombs dropped around them. In the frame of that video, the viewer could not see the planes above, only the running bodies caught within the shaking frame of the mobile phone. In *Shanti* the audience shared a similar point of view: those responsible for the terror remained unembodied, unnamed, and unknown; only the effects of their actions were made visible through the danced movements onstage. Those effects were seen as shared and resulted too, in this multicultural performance not only as a performance of hope and unity as a reaction to the circumstances of war but as a framework for the reaction that is part of the nation and nationalism.

Shanti was a multicultural work within the multicultural arangetram, which abstracted narratives away from histories and contemporary circumstances of inequality "unresolved in the economic and political domains" (Lowe 1996, 30). Bharata natyam (its vocabulary and compositional approach) was a framework for identity and its associated aesthetic qualities to be performed and represented. Through the positioning of bharata natyam as distant and foreign in the arangetram, the dance form became a neutral stage to access ethnic representation. As a modern form built through nation building, bharata natyam was unattached from a specific location to become pan-Asian and universal. It is not surprising that the framework of the dance form would achieve a multicultural usage in Sri Lanka. Historically, the repertoire of bharata natyam was adept to setting movements to lyrics irrespective of the (South Asian) language or religion (Meduri 1996; O'Shea 2007; Soneji 2012). Even *sadir*, the precursor to bharata natyam, incorporated several languages, faiths, and political demands of South Asian kings and British colonists (Soneji 2012).

Shanti performed publicly a multicultural approach to Sri Lanka's war, using markers of ethnic difference—language and religion—defined and rigidified through the mechanism of war. The war had fused language and religion to identity and belonging. Even though the relationship between Sinhala and Buddhist identities is—in archaeological and ancient textual evidence—closely associated but not the same, the contemporary state upholds that "Buddha himself entrusted the island's destiny to the Sinhala people as guardians of his teaching" (Spencer 1990, 3). The state melded religion to itself and positioned Sinhala people as both a minority within South Asia and a majority within the Sri Lankan state and the inheritors and defenders of the island nation. The use of ancient yet contemporarily practiced religious enunciations, *Om shanti shanti shanti* and *Buddham saranam gacchami, dhammam saranam gacchami, sangham saranam gacchami*, successfully tied the identities of the two representatives of the Sinhala and Tamil communities—Anushka and Shankari—to both antiquity and the present-day through the respectable frameworks of spirituality offered in bharata natyam and the accepted frameworks of difference and visibility recognized in multiculturalism. The use of the word *shanti*—a Sanskrit term frequently used in the Hindu context as a hope for peace and a prayer, is not similarly used in the Buddhist one, and thus the title evokes distance and neutrality from the actors and identities that are the focus of the choreography.

The multicultural approach to dance was not unique to *Shanti*. This approach was similar to the collaborations danced by Kandyan and bharata natyam dancers; works often structured as a *jugalbandi* with a back-and-forth rhythmic exchange between dancers.[21] Yet these choreographies clearly saw Kandyan and bharata natyam as distinct markers of Sinhala and Tamil identity, respectively. The forms were brought together on one stage to demonstrate a mutual language of movement. It fit the suggestion of Asha and Naveen at the Fulbright audition. But *Shanti* was unique in its employment of bharata natyam vocabulary to stage both identities mutually.

For *Shanti* Chandran hired an additional singer, who sang the Sinhala lyrics and the Buddhist invocation. He stood next to the seated Carnatic orchestra, holding a microphone in his hand. When I met her after the performance, Chandran stated that the Carnatic musicians were nervous about pronouncing the Sinhala words in *Shanti*. Most Carnatic musicians learn a repertoire of several languages, including Sanskrit, Telegu, Tamil, and Kannada; my own guru in the United States frequently asked musicians to sing North Indian songs, rationalizing that Carnatic and Hindustani music styles share many *ragas* (musical scales) between them. Knowing these many languages, most Carnatic musicians are able to manage broad language and style variances, so I was surprised at the hesitation of these Colombo-based Carnatic musicians to perform these two pieces. The musicians, who were fluent in spoken Sinhala (but perhaps not literate in the language) were not confident enough to sing Sinhala lyrics and were unwilling to perform the Sinhala songs misaligned with the applause that erupted when Anushka and Shankari spoke the language of the Other.

The experience of nervousness, the opposite experience of trust, effectively reminded me of tales where language became a means for testing one's identity and determining one's life or death during riots that hit the country (Jeganathan 2003). The fear to overstep an observed boundary of ethnic identity demonstrated the ways in which multiculturalism undoes how bodies interact with one another. The framework of multiculturalism keeps such representations separate and "equal," when in fact the practice of living, performing, and moving are varied and uneven. Jeganathan states, "Pronunciation is a tactic used in anticipation of a repeat of violence" (2003, 146). The example of "passing" as Sinhala (through pronunciation or accent) was discussed with me several times throughout my time in Colombo. In the space we were—the arangetram—a multicultural setting may have, in fact, created discomfort and fear alongside comfort and hope. Onstage the aesthetics of multiculturalism assisted in disguising the fear and nervousness of the musicians.

The multicultural space of the arangetram demonstrated what Lisa Lowe states is the "institutionalization of unity through acknowledged modalities of difference" (1996, 2). In the schools this is through the difference of arts, language, and religion. In *Shanti* language and religion are juxtaposed. Institutional multiculturalism staged Tamil and Sinhala on equal terrain, and difference in cultures were held as distinct. The explicit comment on the war demonstrated the uniqueness of the interethnic arangetram and its multiethnic audience. It was here that Chandran was able to address the war in more obvious terms.

In the production of the arangetram, Chandran held a different and significant role, as producer. It was her own doing that had forged the event. Because of rising costs of the war economy, fewer and fewer families were conducting arangetrams, and several students had disruptions in their study of the form. Anushka's and Shankari's families were not able to hold an arangetram individually, so Chandran encouraged them to join together for a shared arangetram. Chandran's division of the program, from shared to solo items, allowed both families to have their personal affinities expressed throughout the arangetram.

I met both Anushka and Shankari in person at Chandran's home several weeks after their arangetram. Anushka and Shankari, as sixteen- and seventeen-year-old girls, had experienced Sri Lanka only during wartime. Aside from a short period of relative peace during the Cease-Fire Agreement, they lived through constant hostilities between the LTTE and the government of Sri Lanka.[22] The Colombo in which Anushka and Shankari were growing up was more segregated than that of past generations because of the violence brought by war. Sitting in the front yard of Chandran's home with the warm Colombo sun shining, the girls seemed intrigued by my presence and work but also were confident they had something of value to share with me. I learned that the commonalities between the young dancers extended beyond the dance stage. In fact, both attended the same school but had not known each other (because of the language-segregation policies in Sri Lankan public education) before being introduced by Chandran. Since they both wanted to hold their arangetrams at the same time, and the joint arangetram would split the financial costs between both families, Chandran introduced them. "We met through Miss [their term for Chandran] a year and a half ago for the arangetram," Shankari said. Anushka explained, "We became good friends in dance class. This [dance] leads to a new group of friends that are not my regular friends at school. I'm Sinhalese, and Shankari's Tamil. I know about the fashion of our friendship." I was intrigued by Anushka's use of the word "fashion," as if having friends from various groups or experiences was "fashionable." Considering the segregation of the school system, perhaps it is fashionable.

Anushka expressed how important it was for her to gain an understanding of Tamil culture to perform for the arangetram. She spoke about the difficulties that both she and Shankari "had to overcome" because of her "unfamiliarity with Hindu mythology" common to bharata natyam. She stated, "She [Shankari] would stop after class to explain it to me. . . . I needed Shankari to help me with understanding the Tamil songs." Chandran recognized the effort required by Anushka to learn bharata natyam dance too. She, like several dance teachers who teach in Colombo, noted, "Sinhalese girls work so hard to learn the dance and in fact are better at it." Many Tamil dance teachers seemed more appreciative of the dedication that Sinhala girls demonstrate in crossing ethnic boundaries and learning what they considered a Tamil form. The effort on part of the Shankari to teach and explain Hinduism and "Tamil culture" to Anushka was, however, not something discussed in these conversations.

The two dancers discussed how their friendship emerged, with much of it developing in the dance classroom. Anushka and Shankari were happy with Chandran's decision to create *Shanti* for them. They were glad that it used bharata natyam to make the audience reflect on peace in Sri Lanka. I asked them about their friendship after the arangetram. Although they had spent every day together the month prior to the arangetram, they hadn't seen each other since.

Interpretations of the Momentary

In distinguishing the archive from the repertoire, Diana Taylor discusses how the colonial project discriminated against the repertoire — those ephemeral and performance-based processes (2003, 33). The privileging of the material nature of the archive has been internalized in the postcolonial nation, with the favoring of text, evident in the period of the bharata natyam revival. The privileging of archive material has meant that the repertoire of ephemeral acts is not worthy of theorizing as knowledge, even within Sri Lanka. But movement as meaningful is at the center of dance studies. How it is meaningful demands interpreting layers made unnotice-able, undermined, and ignored through an unqueried acceptance of dance as tradition, as discipline. Here such regimes of discipline can fall under grand narratives of colonization, modernity, and war. Layered meanings may be unknown to the dancers and the dancer-ethnographer, shaped through the disciplinary framework of dance made different, unique, and local through the war in multiple ways.

Attending to the works of Chandran is a project of deciphering nuanced movements—a navigation of time and space not only across the perfor-mance stage by the moving body but in the city of Colombo, which was a site of increasing military presence, invasive and fear-ridden patrols of citi-zens, and shifting access to public spaces. Making sense of the nuance in choreography also demands an investigation in the ways in which these danced pieces draw on larger narratives from the archive. *Draupadhi Saba-tham* draws from the tale of the *Mahabharata* and restages a common ex-cerpt from the epic, a tale known and performed widely. *Shanti* draws from an archival narrative as well, not located in antiquity as the *Mahabharata*, but one that is tied to the rise of the modern nation-state—that of multi-culturalism.

I have suggested that *Draupadhi Sabatham* was a tactic used by Chandran to create a piece about the war in a Tamil space. The choreography's frame-work and the repetition of the story from the *Mahabharata* allowed for an incorporation of the theme of war in a time and place where Tamils were feared in assembly and when Tamil bodies and Tamil spaces were suspect. Although Taylor utilizes the concept of "scenario" to discuss the narrative of conquest and I cannot say that the narrative of the *Mahabharata* is de-ployed similarly among the diversity of South Asians or Hindus, the *Mahab-harata* is a recalled epic, which provides a "portable framework" that "bears the weight of accumulative repeats" (2003, 28). Authorship is attributed to the sage (and actor within the tale) Vyasa, with the earliest parts dated to 400 BCE and its current form to the fourth century CE. The *Mahabharata* is an epic with an abundance of commentary. Historians and Sanskrit schol-ars have argued that the tale focuses on dharma (duty), *shanta rasa* (the emotions and feelings of peace), and equanimity through nonattachment to goals (Dhand 2004; Thapar 2009; Sullivan 2011).

Hindu ideas were later grafted on this text, which was formerly under-stood as a heroic tale that emphasizes equanimity to become a religious text about divine intervention that, conflictingly, emphasizes moral and immoral individuals (Dhand 2004, 48). The text is ridden with self-sacrificing women who act for the necessity of progeny for the clan and nation. The *Mahabharata*, as Taylor's "scenario,"

> makes visible, yet again, what is already there: the ghost, the images, the stereotypes . . . but the scenario predates the script and allows for many possible "endings." . . . The framework allows for occlusions; by positioning our perspective, it promotes certain views while helping to disappear others. (2003, 28)

The "ghosts," "images" and "stereotypes" of the *Mahabharata* as cited through *Draupadhi Sabatham* shows a world divided between good and evil, the wagering of honorable and righteous women and their desire for vengeance, men as women's keepers, and the divine as intervening in humanity yet ensuring war for the sake of it. As a scenario repeated, the *Mahabharata* is cited without much awareness of its criticism in its incorporation in the dance form and repertoire. Its use in an embodied and danced form of bharata natyam reflects the dance's value for the written word. Now the typical bharata natyam audience assesses a performance for quality—the movement of the dancers and the staging. The narrative featured in the form has become expected and understood through the repetition of certain scenes and the occlusion of others. The text and the dance are indecisively detached from embodied and placed understandings. Such "universal" practices, accepted as tradition, allow for a connection to a local context of Sri Lanka's war, especially in a time when public discussions of the conflict seemed impossible and when the audience and organization of such a gathering becomes more suspect than others. Yet through this incorporation of tradition as universal, the audience may or may not detect a connection with the conflict, but the ethnographer and artists on or behind the stage desire such a connection.

Anushka's and Shankari's joint arangetram with the young women who welcomed the guests; the master of ceremony's introduction to the dance form, citing it as ancient and distant; and the evening's program that featured items from the margam repertoire in the first half and solo items that incorporated personal favorites in the second all observed tradition. Yet *Shanti* is considered an innovative piece, unique in its combination and clearly a work created for the moment, the artists onstage, and the audience, in place, in time. The notion of innovation is part of the historical and current practice of bharata natyam. As O'Shea states,

Late-twentieth-century dancers responded to competing demands for innovation and classicism by creating choreography that drew upon historical sources in new ways. These practitioners, like those of the revival, identified as "traditional" an adherence to the values of an overarching, originary form, which they defined in contrasting terms. Dancers expanded possibilities for innovation, however, by drawing upon a wider range of sources than their predecessors had done, located in both historical and living movement practices. A greater specificity in the inquiry into the past combined with an increased interest in creative exploration. Like revival-era dancers, late-twentieth-century performers proposed histories for the dance and suggested means for creating the qualities of a primary form in choreography. These projects provided for new interpretations of bharata natyam's structure and content. (2007, 58)

Shanti, too, draws on traditions and texts "from the archives," combining the framework of bharata natyam's revival that situated the dance as an ancient and spiritual form with the archive of multiculturalism and its political claim for the emerging, modern nation-state through acknowledgment of ethnic and racial difference. Nira Wickremasinghe (2007) considers the Thirteenth Amendment to the Sri Lankan Constitution, which recognized Tamil as an official language, as the official recognition of a multicultural Sri Lankan state. However, she also states that "legislation on language that broadly aimed at using both Sinhala and Tamil in the administration of the country followed but has not been successfully implemented for lack of will and resources." *Shanti* juxtaposed both religion and language through the young Sinhala and Tamil, Buddhist and Hindu dancers. Practices of faith and language were *replicated* in *translation* with each other. Texts were made equivalent to each other and religious practices and emotional states were made the same. *Shanti* utilized markers of ethnic difference constructed in and through war to stage equality. Difference was made equal onstage, while the uneven experiences that mark the terrain of war, such as the "nervousness" among the orchestra, was left offstage. Such unevenness in experience on and offstage parallels the "sites of conflict" within multiculturalism. As Lisa Lowe states,

The terrain of multiculturalism is both a mode of pluralist containment and a vehicle for intervention in that containment. It does not serve our inquiry to attempt to reconcile the narratives or to determine one as dominant. Rather it is in identifying the sites of conflict and antagonism between these different narratives that we reveal the crisis and the opportunities to which the production of multiculturalism responds. (1996, 85)

Lowe's concept of "containment" pushes me to consider how dance and the dancers' bodies are contained by the nation-state's proper expression of multiculturalism. *Shanti* clearly drew on accepted frames of difference—religion and language—and performed them through the bharata natyam form to illustrate a sameness in feeling, hope, and experience. Performing accepted notions of difference within a singular frame of dance, *Shanti* was able to address the war publicly in a time of containment—of bodies, speech, and the combination in subjectivity. The belief of difference and opposition that perpetuated the war and contained identity was opposed and embraced in limited terms by *Shanti*. The segregation in discussing experiences of identity was undone, but only through the acceptable frame of multiculturalism that displayed tolerable cultural signifiers. But these types of cultural signifiers could in fact bring suspicion to the body beyond the multicultural stage. Public spaces, security checkpoints, public transportation, and the streets were places where exacerbated tensions on the battlefield were felt. The experiences of the musicians, the ways in which music was separated, the chosen production by a teacher, a friendship unavailable through segregation in schools, and the "fashionable" aspect of Anushka and Shankari's friendship are "sites of conflict and antagonism" in the different narratives of multiculturalism (Lowe 1996, 85).

I suggest that the audience, along with the bodies performing, shaped the frameworks of the choreography, inspiring the traditional and innovative choreography of Chandran. The mixed audience at the joint arangetram permitted a sense of experimentation and originality. This was in opposition to tradition that confined the Tamil body, illuminated in Asha's question, "Do you dance only to Carnatic music?" or Yogendran's questioning of the imposed cultural sharing of religious practice onstage that ignored the pluralism of the audience. *Shanti* itself is a term that holds different meanings in Hindu and Buddhist theological frames and may illustrate more the influence of U.S. yoga traditions. The title is a demonstration of transculturation that is the mark of culture (D. Taylor 2003, 10).

In looking at *Draupadhi Sabatham* and *Shanti*, my exploration of how (social) space evokes a (social) reality is limited in terms of time scales, focusing on a moment of performance and politics that does not dig *too* deep to uncover layers of change within the particular space of Bishop's College Auditorium or Ladies' College. Through this analysis I explore how notions of tradition and innovation are deployed to protect and promote performance and to protect and promote performers. While tradition has been utilized by the state and nationalisms as a superior value, in performance studies, tradition—although widely understood as an intentionally constructed concept—is considered repetitive and lacking innovation, a failure in an artistry that prizes singular creation. This notion of uniqueness plagues the examination of Sri Lanka within dance studies. Often I am asked, "What exactly is different about bharata natyam practice in Sri Lanka in comparison to the practice in India?" This question not only undoes the constructed nature of modern postcolonial forms bound to the nation-states that demonstrate significant shifts in terms of caste and economic structures but also views traditional performance as an unintelligent, unknown repetition. The predominance of traditional forms are not without warrant or cause; they affectively, and effectively, tie together the subjective, the agentive, and the multiple economics of body, danger, safety, reputation, and beloved and rejected notions of history and future. Both *Shanti* and *Draupadhi Sabatham* attest to creative negotiations within and through frameworks of tradition.

Thus far I have suggested that dance is made through war, as the social space transforms a social reality and vice versa. The ethnographer too is made through research, holding experiences and research that precede the inquiry, the ethnographic process. They are shaped by those around them. When Asha asks if I can "dance only to Carnatic music?" it's not simply an inquiry of values and ideologies but an assessment of a creativity and performance. Dancers and ethnographers are formed by these questions and challenges, these questions of self and actualization. When I noticed the Bharati poem on the TV screen in my mentor's living room, its uniqueness could mark my outsider position, yet in asking the question that an ethnographer must ask—about meaning—I shifted a mundane act to a subversive strategy.

When I returned to Colombo after the end of the war, in 2013, I had the privilege of visiting Chandran at her home. Like usual, we updated each other on shifting living circumstances, the migration of family, and dance—students and events. Over the course of the conversation, I asked about the politics of *Draupadhi Sabatham* and its ties to the local conflict, now over.

Although in 2007 the piece was considered to touch on the war, when Chandran spoke of it again in 2013, her opinion of the work had changed to viewing it as solely traditional and politically neutral. Several questions were raised through this new understanding: Did I misread this work? Was there a failure on my part? Did I, as an outsider, create meaning from the mundane? Was my reading biased and a reaction to the experience of living in the city during the war? I followed up on transcripts to confirm my own knowledge. But I found this shift in our perspectives worthy of analysis—the making and unmaking of meanings of dance, the making and undoing of trust, live experience of the repertoire *contained* through written interpretation. Was neutrality desired pre- and postwar? The revisit and reinterpretation compels me to return to the beautifully written words of Taylor:

> Embodied performance, then, makes visible an entire spectrum of
> attitudes and values. The multicodedness of these practices transmits
> as many layers of meaning as there are spectators, participants, and
> witnesses. (2003, 49)

4

Shakthi Superstar
In Search of Power and Popularity

A clip from each round of the competition was projected on a giant screen before we ascended the stage. Yamini, our choreographer, ran behind the screen, to tell us our cue, which had been finalized just moments before. "Right before the music starts, they are showing a giant countdown clock; start walking onto the stage at two," she instructs with discreet excitement. As we wait for our cue, hundreds of people are flooding into the stadium and filing into the seats. Their shadowed silhouettes morphed with the varied hues of the stage lights. The oversized "movie" clock began the countdown at ten. The audience chanted, "nine," "eight," "seven," with the changing numbers. Attempting to be unseen, we proceeded quickly on the stage, walking up the ramp and taking our positions.

On July 14, 2007, I, along with nine professional Sri Lankan bharata natyam dancers, performed *Title Dance* for the season finale of *Shakthi Superstar*, a Tamil-language, Sri Lankan television show similar to *American Idol*. Beginning with a multiethnic bharata natyam dance, the piece shifted both in terms of choreography and ensemble to meet the demands of the finale's producers. *Title Dance* would incorporate—late in the process— a substantial number of Kandyan-trained dancers to meet the desires of the television program producers.[1] To an outsider the dance may have seemed trivial, but for participants it became a means to make visible and materialize participation in Sri Lankan life and the nation. Even in a choreography produced for popular entertainment and not explicitly or implicitly addressing the war (thematically or metaphorically, like the performances discussed in the previous chapter), dance practitioners read the choreography and their bodies politically. There was a strong desire to curate their movements and visibility on the national, popular stage—affected, in part, by the ongoing war.

Title Dance navigates global circulations of popular culture and civil war. Merging bharata natyam dance and Kandyan dance with "Kollywood" or

Tamil popular cinema, *Title Dance* is a local work and an intricate choreography of approval and refusal of desires and rejections of dance forms and dance styles.[2] The confluence of global forms like Bollywood and Kollywood with bharata natyam and Kandyan dance produces a uniquely local experience. *Title Dance* attempted to insert local representation—including itself as such a representation—rejecting, in part, the popular and circulating practices of Kollywood dance, music, and aesthetics. Resistance to the popular took place in the work of a multiethnic bharata natyam dance troupe, yet associations of ethnicity with dance remained. In considering the locality of this production as a concept, I reflect on Arjun Appadurai's work, *Modernity at Large*:

> I view locality as primarily relational and contextual rather than as scalar or spatial. I see it as a complex phenomenological quality, constituted by a series of links between the sense of social immediacy, the technologies of interactivity, and the relativity of contexts. This phenomenological quality, which expresses itself in certain kinds of agency, sociality and reproducibility, is the main predicate of locality as a category (or subject). (1996, 178)

Considering locality in *Title Dance*, in this chapter I reveal interwoven, intercultural layers exposed in choreography's weaving by dynamics of social relationships and flows of agency and limitation. I write of how war finds its way in the lives, the steps, and the words of dance.

The Beginnings of *Title Dance*

I was paired with Malini on stage right. As the sound of the flute emerged in the accompanying music, she and I, like the two other female dance pairs onstage, rotated around each other, mirroring the other's movements. Pairs of dancers shifted similarly on the periphery of the stage. As the music swelled in volume and in complexity, we and the two other female dancing pairs faced the center of the stage, forming a circle with our hands in *alapadma* mudras as our arms glided toward the center. With steps on our toes, we shifted our weight quickly. In a tight group formed in the center of the stage, we faced the audience, our arms delicately shifting from straight lines to wavelike movements until we posed, again in unison, with our arms encircled above us.

On March 25, 2007, the Tamil Tigers proved to be the first rebel group to build an airplane, committing a nighttime bombing of a military airport near Colombo ("Sri Lankan Rebels" 2007). I arrived at rehearsal the next day to see Kumaran, one of the dancers in our troupe, going over choreography with another dancer, while our producer and host, Padmini, chatted on the phone. As we heard her speak of the bombing the night before, Kumaran started to act out Padmini's conversation through mudras. His right hand in *pataka* mimicked the undetected plane; then quickly both hands formed *mukula* at the base of his gestured scene and, in ripples, shifted to bursting *alapadmas*, imitating explosions. Although several of us listening and watching giggled at the silliness, the ramifications of the bombing were visible around us. There was increased surveillance in the Tamil neighborhood of Wellawatte, where we rehearsed. Armed military personnel ran new and additional checkpoints, stopping individuals as they entered, left, or traveled within the neighborhood, asking them to verify their origins and destinations.[3]

It was just a few weeks earlier that I was invited by Padmini, a well-known artist in the city, to participate in the 150th celebratory episode of *Thimitakata*—a bharata natyam dance competition television series that airs on a local TV station, Shakthi TV. When the *Thimitakata* concert was postponed indefinitely, Padmini decided to transfer all the recruited dancers to another dance on television opportunity, the season finale of *Shakthi Superstar*. The Tamil-language *Shakthi Superstar* and the Sinhala-language *Sirasa Superstar* are Sri Lankan television versions of popular, global singing competitions. *Shakthi Superstar* airs nationally through a privately owned television station.[4]

Padmini, the producer of the dance works for the finale program, was well known for her academic and media work. She is also the founder and director of Padmasri, a multiethnic, Colombo-based dance company. Padmasri creates productions that incorporate several dance forms, reflective of its choreographers and dancers who, in addition to bharata natyam, are trained in other South Asian forms, including Odissi, kathak, or Kandyan dance. This innovative approach makes Padmasri's work especially unique in Colombo since the city is dominated by one particular style of bharata natyam—Kalakshetra bharata natyam. I was introduced to Padmini through my teacher, a retired professor and Padmini's sister. My continuous learning of the bharata natyam technique and compositions through group and private lessons in the city with teachers Padmini knew and promoted and my study under her sister's guidance discreetly provided Padmini with necessary feedback on my dancing and personality. With dancers needed for this specific choreography, Padmini was willing to have me, an outsider, join the group. Aside from me, all the dancers in this initial group knew one another through previous performance experiences. Each of the dancers and the selected choreographer were trained in bharata natyam, most for ten years or more, under various teachers and in a range of Indian and Sri Lankan institutions. Everyone was below thirty-five years of age. Six dancers identified as women: Eashwari, Sharmini, Stella, Malini, Nishali, and me. Four dancers identified as men: Lal, Kumaran, Jeevan, and Rushan. Seven of the dancers and the choreographer identified as Tamil. Three dancers—Rushan, Lal, and Nishali—identified as Sinhala.

As producer of *Title Dance*, Padmini not only selected the dancers but also produced the music for the piece. The music featured her own mix of Carnatic and semiclassical Carnatic tracks, concluding with the final stanzas of the *Shakthi Superstar* title song. But Padmini was not in charge of producing the finale show, only the production of the dance work featured in it. The producers of the finale, Sansuka and Thirana, were Sri Lankan pop stars, whose faces were seen on billboards and TV commercials advertising cell-phone service and milk among other products. As producers, they had given directions to Padmini specifying their ideas for *Title Dance*. They wanted something "less classical" and "more modern." Several weeks after the performance, I had a chance to speak with Padmini about the demands set by Sansuka and Thirana. As we sat one afternoon in her living room, she recalled,

Sansuka and Thirana are like my sons; they are even friends with my sons. But they wanted a Bollywood show. I told them [when they approached me with their ideas for a Bollywood-style show], "[If that's what you want], then I am not the person [to approach]." But [I told them that] I can recommend groups, because the Tamil teachers will not want to send their students. But you *can* ask the Sinhalese groups. Then I mentioned [to them] that we already started choreographing a piece for *Thimitakata* [which was] stopped halfway. They accepted [it]. I also recommended two groups from my university. They [Sansuka and Thirana] saw the kathak [danced at a showing of potential dance pieces choreographed for the concert], and they did not like it because it is too classical. [They] even [thought that] Divya and Sonia's [two other bharata natyam dancers in Colombo who do bharata natyam–Kandyan dance collaborations with Lal] piece is too classical. . . . Even your [group's] item they thought was too classical for that show. I said [to them] "You can't make it lighter than that." But, in the end, they liked the music and the combination with the dance.

Sansuka and Thirana's words illuminate a number of interweaving issues in the production of *Title Dance*: the demands of and desires for popular culture—Bollywood or Kollywood, or filmic music and dance; the resistance to popular culture through aspects of "classical"; and the perception of ethnicized bodies and ethnicized dance and their associations with classical or nonclassical dance. How would a multiethnic bharata natyam dance company address these issues?

Padmini chose Yamini as choreographer of *Title Dance*.[5] Yamini's choreography was conducive to the semiclassical Carnatic music that was our accompaniment. She was able to draw on the tradition yet challenge the rules of the form. Her work was considered more "light" and less classical than "traditional" and "heavy" bharata natyam.[6] At various points in the choreography, the leg movements featured more extensions of the feet and legs and lightly placed footwork that resembled Western modern dance as opposed to the sharp stamp of the flexed foot and the deep angles formed by the diamond-shaped *aramandi* typical in bharata natyam movements. The arm movements were also slower in speed and softer in transitions, allowing curves in the lines of the limbs, unlike the angular, stiff, and quick gestural transitions that cut through space featured in bharata natyam pieces.

But Padmini didn't wish to fulfill Sansuka and Thirana's requests entirely. She was determined to place restrictions on the movements of *Title Dance*. As she stated earlier, Padmini believed that shifting the movements or vocabulary of the piece too drastically would bar her dancers and other Tamil dancers from dancing in the finale, paradoxically preventing the presence of Tamil dancing bodies in this Tamil-language program. Tamil bharata natyam teachers would be unwilling to encourage their students to participate in the show due to its "lighter" elements and visibly less "classical" style of dance. One friend of mine in Colombo, Divya, whom I saw at Shankari and Anushka's arangetram, remarked openly about her decision not to dance in the *Shakthi Superstar* program. When I was chatting with her during the intermission of Shankari and Anushka's arangetram performance, she said that she couldn't be involved with our group because she was trying to be a teacher and "has to maintain a standard" that involves more of "traditional style" of dance. Although Divya participated in several multicultural dances in Colombo that juxtaposed bharata natyam with Kandyan dance, which drew on a familiar frame of the *jugalbandi*, the demands placed on our piece to make it commercially viable and accessible for a large audience exceeded what she could risk in her own dance practice. The ramifications of moving beyond the limits of bharata natyam tradition were both social and economic. If she was viewed as a "less classical" dance teacher she wouldn't be respected in the larger community, and respect(ability) was the commodity that fueled bharata natyam and the classical practices.

There are ironies in the opposition of the classical and filmic; most worthy of discussing here are their associations with each other. Hari Krishnan's (2014) work on Tamil cinema and the role of devadasis illuminates how the construction of the classical took place through the participation of devadasis in early Tamil cinema and their subsequent marginalization from film. Film itself was the mode through which the classical form was created, associated with the divine and the Indian nation-state and a means of replication and production of middle-class values. These themes and approaches would invite women of diverse backgrounds to the dance form. Kareem Khubchandani provides this definition of Bollywood dance, which can describe more regional popular film-dance styles in South Asia:

> Bollywood, a catchall for popular commercial Hindi films coming out of Bombay-based studios, is enjoyed globally as a genre that incorporates song-and-dance sequences. Dance has been an integral part of the Hindi film industry since its inception early in the twentieth century; even the era of silent films featured dance sequences. The long-standing inclusion of song and dance in Hindi film borrows from Hollywood musicals and also signals the early contributions of cultural laborers from Parsi theater, Sanskrit drama, and Persian poetry, as well as professionally displaced courtesans who served as singers and dancers. With the intention of creating a pan-Indian and yet still globally acceptable style, film dance draws widely from classical Indian forms of *bharatanatyam* and *kathak*, rural and folk styles such as *raslila* and *bhangra*, and "Western" popular styles, including salsa, disco, hip hop, and jazz. In pursuit of innovation, Hindi film choreographers have appropriated or mimicked techniques without substantial training; this

makes Bollywood dance a promiscuous form that feels both familiar and alien to those who come to it anew. (2016, 71–72)

Early films boosted the popularity of classical dances like bharata natyam, while bharata natyam was also important to the development and popularity of film and film-dance in Bollywood or Kollywood or other vernacular, popular film genres in South Asia. Television—such as dance-competition shows like *Thimitakata* today in Sri Lanka and previously national initiatives in India—helped popularize the classical dance forms, which were, importantly, assigned as national forms through compulsory programming of dancers' performances (Chakravorty 2006, 123). South Asian filmic music and dance (from Bollywood to Kollywood) are an amalgamation of forms and influences. As S. Theodore Baskaran says, "By 1944 film song as we know it today, with its distinct characteristics had emerged. . . . It was a synthesis of various strains of music, Carnatic, Hindustani, folk and western pop" (1991, 756). Kathak scholar Pallabi Chakravorty states,

One of the biggest forces blurring the fine line between classical/high culture and commercial culture has been Bombay commercial cinema. Although song and dance sequences have been an important feature of commercial Hindi cinema in the past, they have reached new heights in recent years. *Filmee* dance has emerged as an important genre in the metropolitan cities like Bombay and Calcutta, and among the Indian diaspora. It has taken the discourse of innovation to another dimension where new filmic technology has fused with traditional dance techniques to create lavish spectacles such as in the recent mega hit from Bollywood: *Devdas*. (2006, 126)

Chakravorty's (2006) analysis of the demotion of specific kathak practices (courtesan, Islamic, women-based, solo and long-standing abhinaya) and the elevation of others and specific dancers (Brahmin men) as part of the national project demonstrates the national and local governments' interest in constructing kathak as a classical form. Classical and popular-film dance are historically and contemporarily woven. The same judgments against vulgarity and erotic aspects levied against the female dancing body in temples, in courts, and on stages are also levied against filmic dancing bodies on screen.

In terms of *Title Dance*, lines were drawn, negotiated, and redrawn, to keep classical artists in the show by maintaining their respectability as classical dancers (versed in Kandyan, bharata natyam, and kathak styles) and also to maintain a Tamil presence in the show. Irrespective of the mixed composition of the bodies dancing in the piece, Padmini wanted *Title Dance* to be viewed as classical and bharata natyam and received as Tamil. Several times when speaking to us, she would say, "You [and these dancers] are the only Tamil dancers in the entire show" or "This dance is the only Tamil [piece] in the program." Her statements illuminate three observations repeated throughout the process of dance making: (1) Kollywood culture, although Tamil, was viewed as a popular culture of amalgamated forms, especially Western forms, and not considered part of Tamil culture; (2) aside from the seven Tamil dancers, the *Shakthi Superstar* finale contestants, and the masters of ceremonies, all other bodies performing on the stage were perceived as Sinhala, recruited from Sinhala dancing schools; and (3) unlike the *Title Dance* dancers who were featured for one song, the other dancers accompanied several songs sung throughout the finale.

Title Dance demanded explicit transmission of Tamil culture for the sake of figurative and material Tamil representation—a stage further politicized through the uneven experience of war. Although Kollywood songs in the Tamil language are loved by so many within Padmasri and celebrated in the *Shakthi Superstar* finale, according to Padmini, dancing Kollywood was not going to allow for the performance of Tamilness and Tamils. Furthermore, dancing to Kollywood had major consequences within the economy of Tamil bharata natyam teachers—a loss of status and income. Clearly, the ways in which Kollywood could be danced without Tamil bodies threatened the relevance of Tamil dancers (and bharata natyam). It demonstrated that types of representation through movement and language are available, but the bodies may not be.

Sections of the *Title Dance* featured heavier, classically read, rhythmic bharata natyam sequences filled with *aramandi* and quick, flat-footed, rhythmic footwork as well as swift, synchronized, angular leg and arm movements. Although Padmini was an advocate of expanding the scope of traditional bharata natyam through her experimental dance and music productions, the process of creating *Title Dance* for *Shakthi Superstar* led her to limit expanding the movement. She wanted to stage the classical to ensure Tamil identity in the material bodies onstage and in the reading of the dance. We moved, in an ensemble, in waves to the emergent music; we integrated temple sculpture–like poses, but our transitions in and out flowed in and out of unison. We lightly fluttered on our toes as best we could with our little experience with the movement, stretching ourselves straight, foregoing the grounded and weighted moves with which we were familiar. We moved smoothly and softly lifted our legs in various pairings with a soundscape of Western orchestra and Carnatic music. Yamini was finding a way to allow her vision to be danced in spite of recommendations, and she would continuously struggle to maintain this vision with the conditions and perceptions being placed on her work and her dance background. The resistance to the desires of the producers—Sansuka and Thirana—created a clear desire to form her own representation.

Conflict over Costuming in Rehearsals

The increased surveillance on the boundaries of Wellawatte made travel to and from rehearsals at Padmini's house a narrative added to our rehearsals. It was a moment of storytelling upon our entry as we all inquired of one another: "How did you arrive? What happened on the way?" Leaving rehearsal became another layer of choreography as dancers planned an exit—in an ensemble—from Padmini's home. In the dark of night, under beams of streetlamps and a pale wash of light from the moon's glow above us, we walked to the city's thoroughfare, Galle Road, to the specific spots where there was trusted transport home. Only recognized and trusted rickshaw drivers were used to go to and from place to place, and if those drivers were not available, we would walk until we came on another familiar face. Rehearsals were held in the afternoon and typically were not over until after sunset—around eight o'clock. Our meetings were multilingual events. Instructions were most often given in Tamil and informally translated into Sinhala. If there was confusion a voice would yell out, "Translation!"

Rehearsals were where we learned more of Sansuka and Thirana's growing dissatisfaction with the choreography of *Title Dance*. As we continued to learn of the demands of the finale producers, the drive to preserve our classical form to maintain our reputations as classical dancers and, tangentially, as performers of Tamil culture, grew stronger. For some of us, this drive to preserve ourselves was particularly addressed through the visual representations of our dancing woman selves—as classical dancing woman, as bharata natyam dancing woman, as dancing Tamil woman. Although the choreography was still being set, the time had come to discuss costuming, and this particular material visual representation. Clothing became a visible marker that demanded negotiation and agreement.

Two weeks prior to the concert, a showing was held before Sansuka and Thirana at Padmini's home. *Title Dance* was presented that afternoon along with works by other dance groups also asked to perform in the finale. I was starstruck, seeing Sansuka and Thirana sitting among us, no longer just faces on television, storefronts, and billboards. I found myself watching discreetly as they sipped their afternoon tea. I soon realized others were also looking at them, all of us momentarily smitten with the two celebrities. Minutes before we were to show *Title Dance* to the producers, an exchange occurred between Malini and other women in the group. Eashwari, Nishali, and Sharmini criticized Malini for her choice of dress. That day Malini came without the dupatta, a shawl that is tied in front of the chest and around the waist. The dupatta is used a two-fold training tool: it accentuates the dancer's waist visually and internally and reminds the dancer of her waist and weight center; it also adds another layer of cloth in front of the women's chest, a reminder to both the dancer and the viewer of the watched women's body. Dupattas are typically used in bharata natyam practice, as girls mature to teenagers. Adult women wear either a sari or a dupatta with a *salwar khameez*. Several of the *Title Dance* dancers tried to convince Malini to wear a dupatta and encouraged her to borrow one from another dancer, but Malini did not listen. "What will Ms. (Padmini) think? She shouldn't do that," Eashwari whispered to me. "I wouldn't do that," Nishali said. There was no need to explain the concerns over Malini's choice. Everyone understood the criticism and Malini's refusal of being told what to do, but no one wanted to add to an already tense presentation by the group.

After several run-throughs of the piece, we all gathered at the feet of Padmini, as she sat in one of the white molded-plastic chairs in her dance studio. She shared her observations and corrections as an outside viewer, speaking mostly of timing, the lines of our limbs, our faces, our gazes, and the unified and individual movements of the piece. She then proceeded to communicate the producers' concepts for in the show.

She told us that the producers did not want us to look like traditional bharata natyam dancers but to look more "modern" and "contemporary." She asked us to think of costume designs that would make us look more modern. Images of Bollywood dance numbers peppered our brainstorming session. I wondered exactly how our bodies were going to be displayed. I did not want to appear onstage with faux bikini tops like the Indian cinema star and bharata natyam dancer Vyjayinthimala Bali, who would wear costumes that mimicked the garments of celestial nymphs and goddesses found on the walls of Hindu temples: a band of cloth tied around the chest overlaid on a tightly fitted blouse.[7] Of course, Kollywood, Bollywood, and bharata natyam have updated their styles since then, but I understood the term *modern* as the accentuation of women's sexuality, their bust and hips. There was irony in this moment, as Bali helped solidify classical dance as a popular form and even respectable art for respectable women. As we listed costume ideas, we discussed the "seat" of the women's costume or the piece of cloth that wraps around the pants of the common bharata natyam costume, over the hips:

> Malini: We should have gold *busques*.[8]
>
> Yamini: Yes, like a gold sheer organza.
>
> Malini (with a smile on her face): Yes, *akka*, ooh, that would be beautiful![9]
>
> Me (shocked and worried): A gold *busque* would make us look huge, and on television it will be even worse! When we turn around, we will have gold butts! (I didn't know how to respectfully say "butt" in Tamil, so I just said it in English.)
>
> Yamini: Hmm. . . .
>
> [Pause]
>
> Malini (in English): That's true. I didn't think about it, but, yes, it would look like we had gold *bulbs*.
>
> Padmini: Look, she comes from America, and she's so conservative!

Padmini kindly joked about my hesitation to be "modern." Smiling and laughing, she claimed that, because of my concerns with costuming, I must be the "most conservative" of the group and giggled at the paradox of the "conservative" American. My reaction matched textbook analyses of the diaspora. I was deemed at this moment more traditional than those in the homeland. Dorinne Kondo puts forward that those from a diaspora in search of "home" and "haven" is an act of nostalgia that elides exclusion, power relations, and difference; my reaction and participation in the discussion personified her idea (1990, 97). Padmini had her own thoughts of my homes and me. She believed that, coming from the West, I should be willing to show my body or that I would be more open to creating a modern Bollywood piece.

Six days before the *Shakthi Superstar* finale show, Sansuka and Thirana demanded that *Title Dance* feature twenty or more dancers (like a Kollywood number). If we did not want to integrate the additional dancers, *Title Dance* would be cut from the *Shakthi Superstar* finale.[10] Forced to find additional dancers for the show quickly, Padmini recruited dancers from a local university, even though they were trained in Kandyan dance, not bharata natyam. Threatened with being excluded from the program so late in the process and compelled to accommodate more than double the number of participants, we, the dancers in *Title Dance*, were nervous, worried, and hostile. After months of unending changes in choreography, shifting schedules to meet for rehearsals, traveling from distances inside and outside of the city, we were upset by the last-minute request of the producers. The change would require not just reviewing material in the final rehearsals but learning new material. Everyone was already frustrated with the money spent in transport and time and with the seeming lack of appreciation for the work.

Moreover, the difference in our dance training as bharata natyam dancers seemed irrelevant to the process or quality of the piece. We were dancing bodies that didn't display a particular dance form—Kandyan or bharata natyam—but were to mimic Bollywood and Kollywood dancers. The lack of acknowledgment of our training, and the lack of acknowledgment of the training of dancers on film, demonstrated the commodification of dance and dancers as replaceable objects. But the *Title Dance* dancers wanted the labor we had invested to be acknowledged through the performance. We made amendments so that our show would go on.

As we began rehearsals with the twenty or so new dancers, several concerns emerged. Yamini tried to see if the additional dancers could dance sections of the choreography with us in unison. But because of the difference in our training, the new additional dancers were not familiar with the leg and hand movements or the mudras used in the piece. When the coordination seemed too difficult, hindered by the limited number of days before the performance and language barriers (Yamini was versed in Tamil and English, and most of the dancers were fluent in Sinhala), Yamini decided that it would be easiest to separate the choreography between the two groups to keep the newly added dancers at the periphery of our piece—the original *Title Dance*. This way the dancers could conveniently rehearse in separate groups, and the dance styles could remain distinct. She also gave them the task of advertising for *Shakthi Superstar*, by holding banners with the program's name onstage.

For the last showing of the work before the performance, all the dancers convened at National Institute for Sinhala Culture, housed opposite the renowned and massive Bandaranaike Memorial International Convention Hall, the living tribute to Solomon West Ridgeway Dias (S. W. R. D.) Bandaranaike, the fourth president of Sri Lanka. Military personnel were visible on the streets, with security checks placed every few meters on the road; they flagged down cars and asked drivers and passengers for identification cards.

Inside the rehearsal spaces were filled with young men and women dressed in full-body black unitards with shortened sarongs or pleated skirts in solid colors of green or orange, a common practice uniform for Kandyan dancers in the university. Outside there was a concrete slab on which young children were practicing dance steps with their teacher and our codancer Lal, who was instructing the class by playing the steps' beats on the Kandyan drum.

Stepping into the larger auditorium area, we saw Sansuka and Thirana sitting, ready to watch. As I was dancing, my bra strap peeked out beneath my *khameez* blouse. A young Kandyan dancer brought it to my attention as she was sitting in the audience, pointing to her shoulder and gesturing for me to pull my strap inside. It was a noticeable exchange, as my codancer Eashwari shot me a glance. Eashwari commented on the irony of this event, since the other dancers' practice uniform was form fitting—a unitard with a short pleated skirt. All the women dancers in the original *Title Dance* group came prepared with a dupatta for this showing, in which we learned that our piece finally satisfied Sansuka and Thirana's wishes and that we would be included in the program a few days later.

In hindsight I do not believe the producers' aim was to insert Kandyan dance into the program, nor to intentionally minoritize Tamil bodies on-stage. Sansuka and Thirana told Padmini that the program needed to appear modern. Dancing was evaluated on whether it replicated the modernity as presented in Bollywood and Kollywood or failed to do so; there were no distinctions made between Kandyan or bharata natyam dance beyond these dance forms' location on a scale of modernity. Yet Sansuka and Thirana's desire educed an implicit critique within the production of the *Shakthi Superstar* finale. Over and over again the bharata natyam dancing body was viewed as antiquated by outsiders yet simultaneously promoted by insiders as traditional. Janet O'Shea provides an analysis of global bharata natyam dance practice situated among two "competing concerns": tradition and innovation (2007, 22). These competing concerns seem to be compatible with the competing concerns that framed the work of *Title Dance*—classical and modern—but in a local reading what emerged was also a specifically gendered view of local dance practices and their relationships between each other and their dancers and movements.

As antiquity was projected onto bharata natyam from the outside, and through the bharata natyam dancer who was "inside" the form, modernity was conceived as flowing from certain types of heteronormative sex appeal in Bollywood and Kollywood. The modern Bollywood and Kollywood dancer was imagined to be sexually provocative through costuming and dance movements. In her discussion of Kandyan dance, Susan Reed states, "The equation of sexual appeal with being modern appears to be widespread among younger generation stage performers" (2010, 214). Modern was synonymous to sexual, and that type of sexuality was rooted in popular culture that appeared Western—a product of Western influence. The irony is unescapable. The devadasi who danced *sadir* was shamed as a sexual being in the discourse of bharata natyam, a modern discourse tied to nation building. And, as discussed in chapter 1, the colonial project—through Christian sensibilities—covered the colonized with the gifting of cloth, yet in 2007 the postcolonial body covers itself in a refusal to be modern, read as Western. The global domination of Western notions of womanhood, oppression, and liberation shapes a local refusal of the modern in the process of *Title Dance*. It illuminates the complexity of women's beliefs and practices, disavowing the association of sexuality with agency for, as bell hooks states, "Women's liberation was often equated with sexual liberation" in the early stages of the second-wave and Western feminism (2000, 148). Throughout the process of making *Title Dance*, the demands for modern as represented through the popular culture of Bollywood and Kollywood led to a tension felt among the dancers, with the risks to and judgments made of their bodies in displaying or not displaying heterosexist female sexuality. In terms of costuming, women were "in charge" of their own representations, but this privilege was situated in the midst of cultural pressure, among not only the bharata natyam dance community and their fellow dancers but the producers, Sansuka and Thirana.

Our own unwillingness to participate fully in Sansuka and Thirana's demands on us to be modern found a way into our choreography. We, the bharata natyam dancers, relegated the additional Kandyan-trained dancers to displaying the commercial influence on *Title Dance* through their unfurling of the *Shakthi Superstar* banners. In assigning the task of dancing with flags to the additional dancers, we were able to maintain our status as bharata natyam dancers; we did not have to corrupt the form or ourselves by displaying outwardly our commercial sponsorship. Yet the traditional standards that we found ourselves creating and adhering to were entwined with economic rewards. We maintained tradition so that we could be trusted and respected as dancers and dance teachers off the *Shakthi Superstar* stage, *and* we shifted our dancing and accommodated the producers' demands to maintain our presence on the stage. We were in constant flux, through the desires of the audience and through our own desires—or even lack thereof—created through the discipline of dance.

According to Padmini, Kandyan dance students and teachers would be more willing to participate in dancing to Kollywood or Bollywood dance forms. She made it clear that Tamil students would be less willing to dance to Kollywood music. But bharata natyam is also viewed as imposing and influencing the feminizing and sexualizing of Kandyan dance in ways that break from tradition. Reed speaks of "one senior berava teacher" who "criticized the expressive eye movement of one of his best women students as 'bharata natya eyes' inappropriate for Kandyan dance, especially the classical dances" (2010, 214). Bharata natyam as the source of inappropriate movements delineates the ways in which Kandyan dance has shifted to not only popularize the form but also play into specific class and caste dynamics. The femininity in bharata natyam is thought to influence Kandyan dance, making Kandyan dance acceptable for upper-class or caste families:

> Class identity was a significant factor in how dancers articulated what was considered properly feminine. Middle- and upper-class urban dancers were, in general, more concerned about what they viewed as the excessive masculinity of women's dance. Some urban middle-class dancers criticized the berava, suggesting that they were ignorant of the need to "feminize" the dance. The berava dancers, for their part, stressed the importance of maintaining the tradition, contending that the modifications introduced by urban middle-class dancers, such as expressive facial gestures, smiles, and movements of the eyes and hips, were destroying he traditional form. These modifications were seen, in part, as the influence of the emotionally expressive and feminine Tamil form, bharata natyam, which is popular among both Sinhala and Tamil elites in Colombo. (202–3)

A Kandyan dancer who was part of the group of twenty additional dancers in *Title Dance* pointed out a way for me to be more modest at the rehearsal, making note of a shared behavior between our two forms and our two selves. Initially after the exchange, Eashwari and I judged my being told what to do by someone not unknown to both of us, by pointing out the low-neck unitard of the dancer and by competing over how little skin we revealed. Instead of accepting a sameness over practices of modesty and decorum, Eashwari and I invoked a difference between the Kandyan dancers and us as bharata natyam dancers. My own difference as an outsider, a foreigner visiting Colombo and a diasporic Tamil, was effaced through an acknowledgment of my bharata natyam practice and my understanding of certain decorum.[11] Bharata natyam dance practice allowed Eashwari and I, coming from two different experiences, to establish identification between ourselves and find a means of discrimination against another. The pan-Asian aspects of bharata natyam and its influence on other forms or receptivity of influence from other forms was denied in the moment for a stake in differentiating ourselves. We, the original dancers in *Title Dance*, felt threatened by our perpetual state of being cut and definitely in the minority in this finale showing, and we found a way to transform that experience into barring another dancer from claiming respectability.

The threat posed to *Title Dance* was read as a threat to bharata natyam, the presence of Tamils, and Tamil culture in the program. Sansuka and Thirana wanted us to incorporate dancers who had no familiarity with the technique or training, or we could potentially be dismissed from the show. We were told in Tamil that we were the only representation of Tamil in the finale, which urged shifts in movement—and even in our dress on and off-stage—so that we could be read as bharata natyam and not Bollywood, Kollywood, or Kandyan dance. Although there was a specific amount of freedom to break away from the rules and restraints of bharata natyam dance, as a marker of Tamilness, it was a desired and necessary representation. Thus, even within the "liberal and limited terms of representation," this representation was a sought-for form of resistance (Herr 2003, 139).

In the end, *Title Dance* was the only piece that featured a bharata natyam-trained company in the *Shakthi Superstar* finale. We were also the only dance group featuring ethnically Tamil dancers. This felt significant with the escalating conflict. Tamils were literally vanishing—not only on the stage of the *Shakthi Superstar* finale but in the streets of Colombo with the emergence

Our troupe preparing to perform Title Dance. *Photo by the author.*

of the white van syndrome. By the summer of 2007, over a thousand Tamils had disappeared, ambushed by unknown thugs driving a white van, driven away, never to be seen again.

Postconcert Reflections

Sitting with Padmini in her living room, we discuss the recent "disappearances" or kidnappings of Tamil men in her neighborhood of Wellawatte. She recalled an incident over the weekend: "A friend came up to me at a concert the other day, Leela. She was so surprised to see me. She jokingly asked, 'You haven't been abducted yet?'"

Returning the dance jewelry that I rented from the store Fancy Museum, near the Wellawatte bus stand, I ran into my codancer and friend Eashwari. Our ensuing conversation went something like this:

"Hey," she said (always with a smile on her face). I asked her how she had been for the past two days, to which she responded, "I'm all right. Glad it's over."

As I reached in my purse, I asked her, "How do you think it went?"

"Good. Everyone is saying that it was the Tamil part of the show. Once we were done, Tamil culture didn't exist."

"What about all the Tamil songs?" I asked. My question did not seem to raise any reaction or intrigue.

"Ah, yes, but, you know, there was nothing Tamil about the show," she answered.

For several audience members and cultural connoisseurs with whom I spoke after the performance, Tamil culture did not exist in the dance; nor did it exist in the songs (with Tamil lyrics) or the bodies featured after *Title Dance*. They identified Tamil in our dance through our dress and movement. Tamil was performed through our bodies and choreography. We were read as Tamil. Although the process of dance making demanded a semiclassical choreography, Tamilness was identified through the reiterated, frequently cited patterns embedded in the presentation of bharata natyam. South Asian feminist scholar C. S. Lakshmi states,

> When we talk of Tamil identity, however, we are actually talking about the politics of choice; of selectivity; the politics of picking and choosing and perceiving some elements of the culture in a certain way and transforming them into basic elements of an identity. Retention of certain elements in the cultural memory as also the politics of restricting the choice and perception of elements are both open to control and manipulation based on varying power-relations through history. (1999, 58)

Understandings of Tamil identity as limited and exclusive reflect a politics of power and choice. In the responses to *Title Dance*, Tamilness was not located in the Tamil show, the production, or the songs from Kollywood—not by these viewers or dancers. It was located in bharata natyam dance and for Padmini, the dance form and the Tamil dancers. Lakshmi's (1999) statement situates the ways in which agency and restriction are danced through, sidestepped, confronted, and embraced in a nuanced negotiation—charged with power and subjugation, historically and in the contemporary moment. How would Padmini or the original dancers of *Title Dance* perceive their work if there were more Tamil dancers willing to dance to Kollywood on national television? Would Tamilness solely lie in the footwork, stance, pace, gestures, and eye movements of bharata natyam? But such an experience or opportunity was not available in the *Shakthi Superstar* finale for many behaviors and practices that Lakshmi cites: "retention," "politics of restricting the choice," "cultural memory." Padmini's decision to have us represent and perform Tamil culture was political and power-laden, shaped by notions of Tamilness embedded in the dance form, along with gendered and classed practices that deny Tamilness to reside in other twentieth-century and global forms: Kollywood and Bollywood dance.

What interests me in the rejection of Kollywood and Bollywood as Tamil is the rejection of a not so distant kin, the medium that also promoted the form, now a cultural outsider. Both forms, filmic dance and bharata natyam, are iconic and transnational and integral to the visual and embodied creation of the postcolonial. Bharata natyam set its eyes on the past as it was creating itself in the present and future yet was integral to the innovative, boundaries-breaking movement styles of Kollywood and Bollywood that are set in idyllic pasts and imagined futures. The forms are integral to the making of sameness and difference, through repetitive practices of incorporation and rejection.

Kandyan dance's entanglement with bharata natyam also creates undesirable results for some and realized wants for others. Flicks of eyelashes form acceptable femininity that perpetuates an erasure of practices and communities that are the sources of both forms. The training in bharata natyam ensures dancers of their own discernment, their agency in distinguishing correct from incorrect, acceptable from unacceptable. But these evaluations can find themselves in practice and in rhetoric bound to ethnic difference. As Padmini stated, "But [I told them that] I can recommend groups, because the Tamil teachers will not want to send their students. But you *can* ask the Sinhalese groups." Between the willing and permitted dancers onstage are spaces haunted by absence made through patrol and discipline.

As Peggy Phelan states in *Unmarked*, "Representation follows two laws: it always conveys more than it intends; and it is never totalizing" (1993, 2). As dancers for *Title Dance*, we were charged with a sense of purpose through our presence onstage, yet the failures of our presence were felt throughout. The limited freedoms of movement that we did have, the precariousness of our existence, and our smallness in the large production created a sense of separation from the joy and excitement that typically accompanies the popular film–culture experience. *Shakthi Superstar* reifies the popular Tamil culture of Kollywood, which traverses national borders. It might even reify Sinhala Buddhist and nationalist arguments for "barriers of accommodations."[12] But the pan-Asian quality of popular South Asian films—Bollywood or Kollywood—traverse ethnic and national boundaries and borders as well.

Two Sinhala pop stars were in charge of producing the Tamil-language finale in spite of their non-Tamil status. Appadurai's concept of "locality" means understanding the ways in which transnational circulations of cultures, both bharata natyam and Kollywood-Bollywood, can find themselves rubbing against each other to expose differences in power, authority, popularity, and legitimacy. *Title Dance* demonstrates the grating of a desire for a specific local representation of Tamil culture with a transnational one.

As we faded into the dark after our final steps, we let go of the costumes that wrapped our bodies, untying the markers of our presence onstage that didn't even belong to us, rented temporarily from a local jewelry store, the cost of the jewelry too prohibitive to purchase on our own. We dressed in jeans and T-shirts, *salwar khameez*, skirts, and sandals and climbed the steps in the darkness to reach spectators and friends in sections throughout the stadium who were laughing along with the clever masters of ceremonies and Kollywood hits.

Conclusion
Performing Peace

A friend and scholar sent me an email on November 3, 2009, attaching a photo of a billboard she saw located adjacent to the University of Colombo campus. In the corner of the billboard was a stick-figure drawing of a child in shorts and a sleeveless shirt, with chalk-filled circles for eyes and a small, white, oblong mouth verging on a frown. In the drawn child's hands was a red-colored crayon and next to the child was a rifle of the same height with a large red "X" drawn over it. Next to the image was the campaign title, "Bring Back the Child," and underneath, "Stop Child Recruitment." The main image on the billboard was the black-and-white photograph of a girl soldier standing at salute superimposed on the colored photograph of a bharata natyam dancer girl, with the recognizable red-and-green *kanchipuram* sari–like blouse, matching bangles adorning her forearms, and her left hand in *katakamukha* mudra at her chest.[1] The dancing girl's head is covered by the head of the soldier, and her right arm is upward, forming the bent elbow that meets the saluting hand in the black-and-white image. The brow of the girl soldier in the photo is furrowed, her mouth tightly sealed, as she wears a button-up shirt with one collar turned up and the other turned down. The shirt has a disheveled look. It is not the tightly pressed shirt of the easily recollected, global, saluting soldier who appears as a steel-like figure, stoic in expression and ordered in appearance.

In the empty space, next to the dancer and soldier, is the campaign's slogan, "She wants to be a dancer, not a child soldier." And at the bottom of the billboard is a white banner with another message: "Recruiting children is against Sri Lankan and international law. The Government of Sri Lanka has a zero-tolerance policy on the issue." The logos of the sponsors of the campaigns are included at the end of the statement: the Bureau of the Commissioner General of Rehabilitation (an office of the government of Sri Lanka, under the Ministry of Prison Reforms, Rehabilitation, Resettlement and Hindu Religious Affairs) and UNICEF (United Nations International Children's Emergency Fund).

The Bring Back the Child campaign was released on February 26, 2009,

Bring Back the Child billboard at Thummulla Junction (corner of
Kumaratunga Munidasa Mawatha and Philip Gunawardena Mawatha),
in May–June 2009. Photo by Sujatha Meegama.

a time when the war was escalating with great force. "The Dancer," featured
in the image of the billboard and the title of the coordinating commercial
and public service announcement, was part of a series of four commercials
released in the "country's three languages" Sinhala, Tamil, and English. "The
Dancer" is the only commercial featuring a girl; the others — "The Carpenter," "The Student," and "The Cricketer" — feature boys. The announcements
were communicated across Sri Lanka with a concentrated effort in the north
and east by television, radio, newspaper, billboard, and poster. The program
is a collaboration between the Office of the President of Sri Lanka and its
Ministry of Prison Reforms, Rehabilitation, Resettlement and Hindu Religious Affairs and UNICEF to "prevent child recruitment and promote the
release of all recruited children." According to the description, the multi-
media initiative was directed toward armed groups, vulnerable communities, and affected children. In the media release the initiative was financially
supported through the UK Department for International Development and
UNICEF France (Elder 2009). The billboard brought together two ubiquitous
representations of Sri Lankan Tamil girlhood: soldier and dancer.

In partnership with UNICEF and international aid agencies, the government of Sri Lanka spoke to the Tigers' engagement in forced child recruitment through the Bring Back the Child campaign. The Tigers are notorious for introducing suicide bombing to twentieth-century warfare, and women were crucial to this development. The government painted its own image as welcoming to former soldiers of the LTTE — referred to as combatants — through a notion of "No Tolerance" and respect for "International Law" while unveiling, alongside this message, the state-led rehabilitation program. This was in spite of building a coalition with the breakaway faction of the LTTE led by Muralitharan (known as Colonel Karuna), who also subjected children to serve.[2] The government of Sri Lanka did not take on the burden of the reputation of engaging children in war. Instead, the state shaped itself as an advocate for Tamil girlhood, represented through "The Dancer." The ability of the well-known international organization and the state to turn to the image of the dancer in this campaign demonstrates bharata natyam's success in conveying an ideal girlhood. The girl is the dancer, not the cricket player and not the carpenter. And she's not just any dancer, but a bharata natyam dancer.

In the "before" image of the billboard and commercial, the girl practicing bharata natyam is unbroken — she is happy; she is considered "free." But the reality is that she exists in a place and time of war, undeniable through the immediacy and potential of her forced recruitment. The juxtaposition of image and text provides a notion of choice and desire when desires and choices are curtailed by war itself. Discipline and chastity are central to the soldier — women's sexuality is curtailed by militancy (De Mel 2003). Chastity and discipline were important to the success of bharata natyam as a form. I am not wanting here to argue for child soldiers. The histories of the brutality of recruitment in the punishment of families who lived under the areas of Tiger control, and the grief, the courage, and the drive of parents to protect their children, to locate and bring their children home, is a testament to the resistance that continued against a field of violence. The resistance to children being forcibly taken speaks to the diversity (of perspectives, of experiences) that lived under the authoritarian regime of the LTTE and demonstrates a multiplicity often not allowed in conceptions of the Tamil body by the state, which subjected that body to search, surveillance, and suspicion during and after the war.

The Bring Back the Child campaign announced, too, a government program of rehabilitation. Yet alongside the complexity of the Tamil experience, there is complexity in the state. Years after the war's end on May 18, 2009, two images of the twelve-year-old son of Prabhakaran—the LTTE leader—surfaced, allegedly taken in the final moments of the conflict. In one the child sits shirtless in shorts; in the other he is on the grass with clearly marked gunshot wounds on his torso. As critiques of the state's involvement in the death of the child emerged, the state dismissed the allegations, stating they were "lies, half-truths and numerous forms of speculation" (Press Trust of India 2013). Global projects for reconciliation typically are tied to the "exposure of truth" (Ntsebeza, qtd. in Cole 2007, 184–86).

"The Dancer" demonstrates the way in which bharata natyam is utilized by the state as a representation of difference to project onto itself safety and to show a global and local audience its investment in unity and progress. The bharata natyam dancer, as discussed thus far, is embedded in gendered and ethnic imaginings and practices for community. I have often found it as a "happy" representative of Tamilness on multicultural stages and, here too, in this billboard provided by the state. The form evokes unbrokenness, in its early twentieth-century iteration as untainted by the shifts of colonialism and imperialism, and in 2009 it is easily used to stage inclusion and unbrokenness from war. Its deployment in Bring Back the Child evokes an awareness of Tamilness and, along with it, beauty, proper play, and appropriate arts. The use of the dancer conveys globally and locally an understanding of the Tamil experience. As discussed in previous chapters, the bharata natyam dancer is an abundant image that in its transnational circulation navigates concepts and strategies of identification—national, ethnic, gendered, and sexual. The dancer and the soldier are made oppositional in this frame, but the girls are connected by nationalisms, Tamil and Sri Lankan. Returning to Lisa Duggan's notion of multicultural neoliberalism (discussed in chapter 2), I briefly examine here how these cultural works function in tandem with state consolidation and state-based development work (2003, xii).

Visiting with Padmini, 2012

Three years after the end of the war, in May 2012, I returned to see Padmini, director of Padmasri, the bharata natyam dance troupe with which I performed the *Shakthi Superstar* finale. I would learn that in the war's final months and period immediately following, her company would be asked to perform throughout the country as a means of engaging in international diplomacy between nations. The criterion placed on her engagement reveals values for inclusion held closely by the government of Sri Lanka along with perceptions of the government held by foreign governments. Seeing Padmini, I noticed that in the in-between, much had shifted for her. She was now living alone—all of her children had migrated abroad.[3] Her health was failing, demonstrated in her slow and cautious walk and in the tremble of her left hand. Her dance company was more firmly established than it had been five years earlier. She was now involved in various performance projects coordinated after the end of the war, several of which addressed ethnicity in postwar Sri Lanka. These new projects, funded by NGOs, diplomatic missions, and the state, had been filling her calendar and demonstrated a developing role of the arts and bharata natyam practice in postconflict Sri Lanka. One production, of which she spoke at our meeting, was sponsored by the Indian High Commission.

The piece was set to a Carnatic music score and Tamil lyrics composed and written by Padmini herself and was initially to be debuted in mid-2009. But as the war came to an unexpected and brutal finale in May that year, Padmini was soon approached by the Indian High Commission to change the piece.[4] They wanted the production to be set to Sinhala lyrics and not to Tamil, as a gesture of "good faith" and "respect" for the Sri Lankan government. The Sinhala-language production was marketed as a reflection of the bilateral relationship between India and Sri Lanka. The shift of language to appease the government was in line with India's emerging relationship with Sri Lanka. During the final stages of the war, India did not act as a conflict manager. Instead, as it had from 2007, India quietly supported the Sri Lankan government's offensive against the Tigers, marking a major shift from its previous role as "peacemaker" and covert supporter of the Tigers in the 1980s and its public "hands off" policy pursued since 1991 with the Tiger's assassination of Rajiv Gandhi (Destradi 2012, 596).[5]

As we sat in her living room, Padmini recalled being asked to switch the language of the production and hinted at the discomfort it brought to her:

> They told me that the Indian government wants us to do their Indian dramas in the language of the host country. People were angry that I did it in Sinhala. I didn't even tell my sister—how could I tell her that I was doing this in Sinhala? People would wonder why I'm doing that, and whether I'm doing this to "butter up" the government.

Padmini feared the backlash of setting the production to the Sinhala language. Her uneasiness arose in part to the speculation of human rights violations, the large number of Tamil civilian casualties in the months surrounding the end of the war that May, and the massive quantity of internally displaced persons relocated to camps, one of which held more than 225,000 people (Perera 2012).

The status of Sri Lankan Tamil people continued to be in flux even after the war, and Padmini feared being read as a sympathizer for either side—the Tigers or the government—a reflection of the ideologically divisive war that offers little space for the in-between. She asked a Sinhala colleague and fellow professor to write the Sinhala lyrics, and a Sinhala student of hers, who was studying Carnatic and Hindustani music, also assisted. She later stated, "When people watched, they said they didn't worry about the language. Most of the production was in Carnatic style, the abhinaya and the mudras are the same, so why worry about the language?" The production included Kandyan dance. In one section of the work, several recognized Indian classical dance forms—kuchipudi, odissi, and kathak—were featured. The practice of the body, highlighted in her acknowledgment of the gestures and facial expressions, were considered important to maintaining a presence of bharata natyam.

The Colombo performance of the drama in Sinhala was a success, and the Indian High Commission asked Padmini to then stage the Tamil-language version of the production that she originally composed, in Jaffna ten months later, in May 2010. But when Padmini wanted to stage the Tamil version in Colombo one month after the Jaffna production, the High Commission would not provide financial assistance. Padmini instead sought funds independently and obtained them through the Norwegian Agency for Development Cooperation). The three performances were accompanied by three different written programs, which varied. The program for the first performance, in Sinhala, mentions a blending of Indian classical music and dance styles. The second performance, in Tamil, mentions only Carnatic music. The third program, in Tamil, mentions that Carnatic and Hindustani music were incorporated. However, both programs for the Tamil-language productions do not mention the Sinhala-language performance, nor does the program for the Sinhala-language production mention its translation from Tamil to Sinhala. The program for the Tamil-language production in Colombo, although mentioning of Hindustani music, does not divulge the Sinhala-language production. Notably, the Tamil-language versions of the production did not include the Kandyan dance troupe.

For Padmini, this was her first time doing a production entirely in Sinhala, even though she is fluent in the language. It was also her first visit to

Jaffna since the end of the war—one that left a significant impression. She told me that the production attracted a packed and appreciative audience but also caused her some sadness. "We actually stayed in a hotel," she said. "Before, when [my family] visited, there would always be someone there to take care of us. We would never think of staying in a hotel—our whole community was there—but now no one is." Her words highlight the shifts within her family, with most joining the hundreds of thousands that make the Sri Lankan Tamil diaspora.

The productions expose the politicizing of dance, land, language, and the segregation, if not management, of each. The productions also speak to the labor of dancers for development, nation building, and international diplomacy. Padmini wanted more than was asked of or granted to her: she wanted to be allowed to share her work in Colombo again, and she wanted to be seen in the many communities with which she called home. In a hybrid sense she played with form and space in search of belonging.

Although approached by the Indian High Commission to stage—with conditions—a production for the sake of diplomatic relations between India and Sri Lanka, Padmini would not be approached by the Sri Lankan government to perform in the grand opening of the Nelum Pokuna Mahinda Rajapaksa Theatre in Colombo on December 15, 2011. Named after the then president of Sri Lanka, Mahinda Rajapaksa (2005–15), the state-of-the-art theater cost 3,080 million rupees (approx. US$308 million). Like most donor projects funded by the Chinese government, the theater was considered an "infrastructure-based project." China covered 80 percent of the theater's cost and gifted most of the building materials (Prins 2011).[6]

The National Theatre, as it was previously known, was under the Ministry of Culture; immediately following the war, Nelum Pokuna's administration was transferred to the offices of the president and the presidential secretariat. Its administration, security, and upkeep were transferred to the three armed forces: the army, air force and navy (Prins 2011). The theater's opening was marked by a grand, televised ceremony filled with a parade of Kandyan dance performances to welcome the president, dignitaries, and guests. A Kandyan dance drama and Chinese ballet were the first performances on the new stage. Although Padmasri was not asked to perform, as a recognized artist, Padmini was invited to the opening celebration and asked to provide a written felicitation for the program. In her letter she expressed her vision for the performing arts in postwar Sri Lanka:

This opening ceremony could not have come at a better time when concerted efforts are being made to revive the rich cultural traditions of the performing arts in the country. Of recent, the felt need for reviving such preservations peaked at the Jaffna music festival held in Jaffna in late March 2011 wherein Sri Lanka's rich and varied folk art forms were presented by several groups representing all ethnic communities from all regions around the country. . . . This new theatre I am certain, will take upon the noble task of reviving and preserving all forms of the performing arts and evolve eventually into a meeting point, to foster and build a strong foundation for the indigenous traditional cultural legacies to flourish for the benefit of the future generations.[7]

Padmini's felicitation puts forth a desire for the theater to be a meeting point between all forms of the performing arts. She deploys a vision of the arts as an archive constituting a cultural legacy for future generations and implicitly invokes the ethnic divisions that form part of that legacy in her reflection on the music festival (which was funded by the Norwegian Agency for Development Cooperation) that took place in Jaffna, the embattled and symbolic city. She reads this event as a site for preserving "indigenous" legacies—a word employed in the early experiences of bharata natyam—and uses the word to inscribe the city, its people, its arts, with belonging. The opening celebrations of Nelum Pokuna Theatre disappointed Padmini; her words were included but her arts were not. She felt that the exclusive staging of Kandyan dance did not represent Sri Lanka at this crucial moment. She laughed as she recalled the moment when a senior member of the president's office asked her about the program. In response she openly told him, "I don't believe it represented Sri Lanka, and I am disappointed at the lack of diversity. Please inform the president of my thoughts." The aide replied, "Don't worry, madam, he already knows." Her laugh conveyed her acknowledgment of state surveillance.

Neoliberalism and Homes in Postwar Sri Lanka

The differences between my stays in 2007, 2009, and 2012 were many. In the first visit Wellawatte was encircled by military "security" checkpoints. Reverberations of violence in the northern and eastern battlefields were palpable in the neighborhood where Padmini's home (and our rehearsal space) was located. Additional checkpoints often popped up overnight, as the war escalated to its final phase, and soldiers frequently stopped individuals as they entered, left, or traveled within the neighborhood, and they questioned residents of their origins and destinations.[8] When I visited two years later, in February 2009, the explosion of war in the north demanded soldiers from all regions of the island, and security checkpoints throughout the city were left largely abandoned. Known tragedies were taking place just hours away, but residents of the city could move with more ease in the absence of policing.

Within the first five months of 2009—inclusive of my short visit to Colombo—an estimated 6,500 people died in the conflict ("US Calls"). In the final months of the war, accusations were waged against both the Tigers and the Sri Lankan army for using civilians as human shields, as the two warring parties surrounded a narrow strip of land on the eastern coast filled with hundreds of thousands of Tamils attempting to escape the war (Sengupta 2009). The war was declared over in May 2009 with the killing—execution style—of the Tigers' leadership (Ethirajan 2009). It was an unexpected end to a twenty-six-year war that generations had experienced and believed would continue indefinitely. When I returned to Colombo three years later, in May 2012, travel in three-wheelers on roads clear of checkpoints made late-night life easier. Wellawatte, the neighborhood central to my former dance community, was no longer encircled by checkpoints or burdened by routine and unexpected searches in the middle of the night.

In discussing dance during war, I have shown how artists and the state manage the form's hybrid and transnational history and contemporary practice. I propose that dance can address and define ethnic identity in ways that reject the hybridity that informs the practice, that dance is given a desired symbolic value that hides undesired bodies, and that dance can be a means of inserting bodies to ascribe them value. Cultural nationalism shapes identity's value or its rejection. Minority representation is used to build material and diplomatic capital for the state. As international NGOs, community-based organizations (CBOs), and diplomatic missions have been intervening in the war and continue to do so by investing in postwar development, their efforts, in tandem with the states and other actors, continue to shape bharata natyam and its practice and meaning. As a recognizable marker of "Tamilness," bharata natyam is being used and deployed as a useful marker of Tamilness in postwar productions. Through this representation of difference, the state projects onto itself safety and belonging. This focus on women's agency is also part of the trend in neoliberal development projects that funnels large amounts of funds to focus on women's education and productive value under a guise of individual empowerment and feminism.

Emerging from a war through a government-led defeat of the minority separatists, by and large, the state was critiqued for focusing too much on regime consolidation under the majority, predominantly Sinhala government (of the Rajapaksa government, the former president of Sri Lanka) (Uyangoda and Jayawardena 2010). According to Jeyadeva Uyangoda's (2010) summary for *Asian Survey*, at the end of 2009 there were upward of three hundred thousand displaced Tamil civilians and a government reluctant to resettle them, as well as rising tensions between the Sri Lankan government and Western powers (the United States, European Union, and United Nations) over human rights violations and war crimes. At the same time of the publication of Uyangoda's summary, however, the *New York Times* listed Sri Lanka as the number-one destination in its list of thirty-one countries to visit in 2010 (Beehner 2010). There was a strong connection between the "war for peace" and the "post-war" periods (Goodhand 2012, 130). The government pushed for rapid economic development in the north and east of the country, but some saw these initiatives as bolstering state security and military power to prevent a reoccurrence of Tamil militancy. Jonathan Goodhand describes the north and east as in a "state of emergency" in 2011, settled by a high number of military personnel and excessive rates of violence—abductions, sexual assaults, and killings (2012, 133).

Although there was pressure from Western countries to investigate the issue of war crimes, the Sri Lankan government strengthened its ties with China, India, and Japan, who had a hands-off policy when it came to the country's domestic affairs (136). Furthermore, state-led rehabilitation programs, like the Bring Back the Child campaign, aimed for the rehabilitation of "misguided" men, women, and children. The official website of the Bureau of the Commissioner General of Rehabilitation (an office within the ministry) states the following in its introduction:

> The government of Sri Lanka headed by HE [His Eminence] the President who is guided by the Buddhist principles of forgiveness and compassion knowing the value of human life, thought that, as the terrorists are human beings whose minds were distorted, and hence misguided, [they] could be reformed and could be rehabilitated to

enlist their services as useful citizens of the country. For this purpose, he sought the assistance of the very Security Forces which led a humanitarian war against the terrorists.

In contrast, in other countries where terrorists had been active and when they were detected and captured they were summarily killed as they work on the presumption that they cannot be reformed and rehabilitated. In order to ensure their destruction, they were shot on the head leaving no chance of survival. Apart from human considerations, Sri Lanka cannot afford to lose the lives of valuable human beings as Sri Lanka is increasing its population at a decreasing rate. (Bureau 2011)

There are specific wordings that I emphasize here: the state identifying itself as Buddhist and compassionate; the conflict as a "humanitarian war"; the labeling of LTTE members as terrorists (even though forced recruitment is acknowledged in the Bring Back the Child campaign); and *not* summarily executing members of the LTTE as a demonstration of a compassionate state. The bureau's mission is to ensure reintegration and reconciliation through rehabilitation.

Reconciliation often upholds notions of democracy in the emerging nation as an antithesis to the nationalist project that preceded it (R. Wilson 2001, 2). Reconciliation is typically tied to the exposure of truth (Cole 2007). Atrocities and violence that marked the final months of the war continue to be revisited and analyzed in search for the truth. Three years after the end of the conflict, the United Nations declared its own failure in fulfilling its mandate to protect civilians during the last months of the war (Gamage 2012). A U.S.-led resolution to investigate potential war crimes was passed in March 2013 (Cumming-Bruce 2012). In discussing the creation of a new constitution and a transitional justice system that would help address the schism from the war, the current government engaged in collecting thousands of testimonials, but there continues to be the fear that such mechanisms are only for show and not for change. As Smriti Daniel (2017) states, "Sri Lankan activists will tell you that the island has a commission culture," where in the past fifteen years "thousands have testified and thousands have been disappointed by how little has changed despite their courage."

Catherine Cole states that truth is found in the "unscripted" and "unexpected" (2007, 186). On July 16, 2016, violence broke out in the campus of the University of Jaffna, as students clashed over the inclusion of Kandyan dance at the opening ceremony for the faculty. According to an article by Laksiri Fernando (2016) for the *Colombo Telegraph*, the student committee of the science student union had planned a convocation ceremony with Tamil drums and music. The Sinhala students put in a request for the ceremony to have Kandyan dance in the procession as well. The committee then passed it on to the larger University Students Union, which incorporated arts and management students, who then rejected their request, insisting that only the Tamil welcome form should be allowed. Faculty attempted to appease the conflict by doing away with the march and having only music inside the hall with the two types of welcome rituals. However, according to reports, Tamil musicians showed up at the gate ready to start the procession, and the Sinhala students urged the Kandyan dancers, who were prepared to dance inside the hall, to join the march. At that time Tamil students—supposedly from the divisions of arts and managements—reportedly threw stones at the Sinhala students. The university authorities brought in buses to send the Sinhala students to their homes in the south. Two weeks later the students still had not returned.

In the reactions to the event, there are charges that the event was a "violent staging of Kandyan dance"; that Tamils and Tamil areas are ethnically restrictive, unlike Sinhala areas and Sinhala people in the country; that arts and management students were more discriminatory than science students; and that the military urged the students to ask for Kandyan dance. The conversation sparked discussions of the militarization of Jaffna, the composition of security on the peninsula, and the role of culture as a "uniting factor compared to the language" (Fernando 2016). I see truth emerging here, in the ruptures, in the many interpretations, like I see it in Padmini's navigations, her critiques, her adjustments, and her disappointment. These continue to shape her work and her presence onstage when invited and even offstage as an observer and commentator.

Over the course of its practice in Sri Lanka, bharata natyam has been shaped to project Tamilness—alongside this, a sense of foreignness—and in the postwar era a representation of benevolent inclusion within the hybrid nation. Its deployment evokes an awareness of a minority community. In unpacking this "awareness," the Tamil people are broken in two: neutral citizen or militant terrorist. The life experience contradicts the staged or visual representation of the bharata natyam dancer. The dancer in the billboard and the dancer onstage become frozen, not in the either/or of safety or fear but through an awareness of the complex transnational circulation that demonstrates a practice of strategic navigation—national, ethnic, gendered, and sexual.

The contradictions in the practice of bharata natyam are twofold: the rejection of the popular although the popular was the means to create the form and the rejection of nation and ethnicity even though such identifications are part of the formation of the practice. Utilizing ethnography, this work has used the embodied practice to consider political maneuvers and how both inform each other. As Butler suggests, "There can be no radical politics of change without performative contradiction." My aim in this text is to pursue embracing and recognizing the contradictions to further a more radical politics of understanding dance practice (Butler and Spivak 2007, 66).

There, Here, Then, Now

I reflect often at what cost my own representation (as a South Asian, diasporic, dance scholar who works on transnational circulations of culture) is deployed in an North American academy somewhat struggling to see significance in Sri Lanka, whether that's due to the cultural and intellectual presence of India globally or in the ways in which ethnicity takes on currency—materially and intellectually—when in relation to white subjects and through placements in North America or Europe. Both of these potentials are composed of a projection rejected in postcolonial studies yet somewhat still at hold within the Western academy. Thus, India, as a force of cultural and political dominance within Sri Lanka and the root of significant culture globally, can reflect a projection of culture that is a static condition. Ethnicity as understood as worthy of study through its relation to, or rejection of, the whiteness of settler colonialism provides a field of study that is academically relevant and powerful yet can dominate over the nuances of ethnicity that exist in places excluded from popular trends of neoliberal multiculturalism.

My conclusion is marked by shorter exchanges with artists, along with more analyses of images and events from afar. My visits with the artists and mentors mentioned in this text—who had become friends and guides—were limited since 2007 through my own condition of temporary, sessional work in the academy. The economic crisis of 2008 in the United States further entrenched the education landscape with temporary workers who took on more than full-time teaching loads for minimal pay. I completed this text while working on a long-term, contractual basis in a newly created, penultimate neoliberal vision for higher education in Canada, where provisions for research and inclusive and equitable practices (structural support) have been dismissed through a constant drone of financial restrictions on the university and its workers now, which will be solved through future opportunities in real estate–based developments. The individual educator's scholarship and teaching, accomplished in spite of cutbacks, is often transformed into an act of collegial work ethic and valued friendliness and understanding. There is unevenness of power within the academy.

The unevenness of power distributed across paths of intellectual analysis only furthers the necessity of rigorous study of this unevenness, as in Bhabha's words: "The incommensurability of cultural values and priorities that the postcolonial critic represents cannot be accommodated within a relativism that assumes a public and symmetrical world" (1992, 48). As a diasporic scholar of Sri Lankan background, my own body is implicated in a relationship according to the values ascribed to it, in and outside of the academy.

In discussing the protests that took place in Canada in the final months of the war between the government of Sri Lanka and the Tigers, Ahilan Kadirgamar claimed,

> Indeed, given Sri Lanka's lack of geopolitical significance, the political will of western actors is unlikely to change with or without the lobbying of the Tamil diaspora. Rather, engagement with the Tamil diaspora has only become an extension of the diplomatic and rhetorical tools that western officials have been, so far, willing to use to pressure the government of Sri Lanka on certain humanitarian and human rights concerns. (2010, 25)

Kadirgamar's (2010) analysis demonstrates the limitations imposed on the diasporic community, as valued through the appropriation of values of the state. I appreciate the willingness to minimize the diasporic subject as a means for greater human rights interventions. And such human rights interventions, too, are also shaped by the rejection of the diaspora and the unwillingness to keep borders open to allow for more refugees from war to arrive. Mandates for Western intervention are sometimes created through the rejection of Others' bodies by, and in, the new home. Can war just stop so people can stay and not flee?

One of the learning outcomes at my institution is "International Perspectives," and a colleague sent me an email suggesting that he does not know what the phrase means. His email poked rhetorically at the faculty who do teach about and do work elsewhere to justify its importance. Here, too, I seek belonging. I end this writing, for now, questioning the usages of such representations in neoliberal conditions in the many places that have provided me a home, albeit uncertain ones. As I turn my eyes to the artistic landscape of postwar Sri Lanka and glance at emails sent from British Columbia, I leave considering the transnational intersections of places there, and here.

Notes

Introduction

1. Carnatic music is a genre of classical music from South India.

2. Ganesha is the elephant-headed god widely known in Hindu religious practice. As a remover of obstacles, he is worshipped by Hindu believers at the start of any endeavor or undertaking. In Sri Lanka Ganesha is featured not only at Hindu *kovils* or temples but also in Buddhist ones. He is popular among many Sri Lankans and adorns homes, vehicles, and stores throughout Colombo.

3. Mudra is a stylized hand gesture used to convey lyrics, and in theatrical or dramatic phrases it conveys specific meanings. *Ardha chandra* mudra is a hand gesture where the fingers extended together and the thumb is extended perpendicular to the palm. Meaning "half-moon," *ardha chandra* is used here to connote Lord Ganesha's flapping elephant ears. *Aramandi* is a half squat, the foundational leg position in bharata natyam.

4. *Alapadma* mudra is a hand gesture where the fingers are spread in a wave; it means "fully bloomed lotus."

5. The *vannam* is a form of dance within Kandyan-dance training and repertoire. *Vannams* were developed from the ritual kohomba kankariya and became integrated within the Kandyan-dance syllabus (Reed 2010). Most describe the behaviors of animals, including elephants, monkeys, rabbits, and peacocks.

6. Tamil identity has shifted over time socially and politically. In the Sri Lankan context Tamil has meant the Tamils from Sri Lanka, distinguished from Malaiyaha Tamils brought over during the British colonial period. Tamil culture and identity, as shared between Tamils of Tamil Nadu and Tamils of Sri Lanka, have also shifted from a perspective of one shared culture to distinguished cultural identities. For an articulation of the complex and hybrid nature of Buddhist and Hindu practices in Sri Lanka, see Tambiah (1992) and Pfaffenberger (1979).

7. The war was declared over with the killing of the Liberation Tigers of Tamil Eelam (LTTE) leadership, including the head of the organization, Vellupillai Prabakharan, on May 18, 2009.

8. The island was a site of foreign invasion by several Indian rulers and an island shaped too by Arab traders over many centuries prior to European colonization—first the Portuguese (1505–1658), then the Dutch (1658–1796), and then the British (1815–1948).

9. I would be remiss to not mention the LTTE's forced removal of northern Muslims from the Northern Province in October 1990. The expulsion of almost eighty thousand Muslims from the province was argued as a response to the increasing opposition by Muslims to the establishment of a separate Tamil homeland.

10. See also Rogers (1990); Nissan and Stirrat (1990); and Gunawardena (1990).

11. Quoting Gyan Pandey, Jayawardena and de Alwis state that communalism means the "advocacy of violence" (1996, xvi–xvii). Jayawardena and de Alwis are interested in how the advocacy of violence is often targeted sexually toward the "Other's" woman. I use

the term *communalist* to connote not only violence but also a cultural reshaping that does not allow for differentiation within community.

12. Bharata natyam also has significance among the Sri Lankan Tamil diaspora. Examining works by Sri Lankan Tamil choreographers in Canada, O'Shea illuminates that bharata natyam can be meaningful in demonstrating Tamil identity and has been choreographed to "demonstrate the need for a separate nation-state based on linguistic and ethnic commonality" (2007, 102). Her examination of bharata natyam dance works that have obvious connections to the Tamil nationalist militant group, the LTTE, shows the dance form's significance among distinct Sri Lankan Tamil communities. Ann David (2008) has shown that within the British Sri Lankan Tamil community, dance is a means of retaining Tamil identity and has been incorporated into Sri Lankan Hindu Tamil religious and devotional practice.

Chapter 1

1. Jatiswaram and *kirtanam* are two compositional styles in a bharata natyam concert repertoire.

2. Cinnamon Gardens, also known as Colombo 7, was the home to some of the most privileged and elite families of Colombo. Shyam Selvadurai's (1998) fictional novel, *Cinnamon Gardens*, examines the community of these professional families, who were not only vanguards in terms of education but also very conservative in terms of family values, social status, and religion. Although it is a fictional account, Selvadurai's novel provides an engaging descriptive account of life among the Colombo elite.

3. For more on ethnography and the fictive ethnographer, see Visweswaran (1994).

4. Jaffna was the second-largest city in Sri Lanka prior to the civil war, and its cultural influence and economic presence in the history of Sri Lanka was highly desired during the war. The peninsula was constructed as a "physical and ideological battlefield of Tamil nationalism" (Thiranagama 2011, 15). Although the war would move eastward over its course, Jaffna continued to be viewed as significant because of the domination of Jaffna Tamils in the nationalist movement throughout the twentieth century (Tambiah 1986, 1992; Pfaffenberger 1994). Furthermore, East Coast Tamils were concerned that the separatist state would be controlled by Jaffna Tamils (Pfaffenberger 1994; McGilvray 1998, 2008).

5. The culture of Jaffna Tamils and "Vellalar domination" is important to this discussion, as most Tamil practitioners in the early years were identified as Jaffna Tamil. Although the community discussed in the following pages includes Tamils who identify as East Coast Tamils, Tamil bharata natyam practice continues to be dominated by the Jaffna Tamils.

6. Krishnan (2014) also illuminates in more detail the role of film in the revival of Bharata Natyam dance. Devadasis were the earliest actors in Tamil cinema, yet, over the growth of film and nationalism in the early postcolonial years, Devadasis would be marginalized through upper-caste women who became the known dancers that brought bharata natyam into the households of middle-class Tamil families. Thus, film too was integral to the creation of a pan-Asian form of bharata natyam, and Brahmin women dancers were part of this promulgation of the dance. The role of Tamil cinema in bharata natyam practices in Colombo is discussed further in chapter 4.

7. *Nattuvanars* are male dance masters that trained devadasis in the dance form. For more on their role in temple dance practice and in the revival, please see Kersenboom-Story (1987); Meduri (1996); and Soneji (2010, 2012).

8. I would learn from my colleague and South Asia studies scholar, Phillip Friedrich, that this Nikaya was initially inclusive and conceived of itself as a refuge for the down-trodden and vulnerable. It was formed because the casteist Kandyan Siyam Nikaya would not allow the non-Goyigama Sinhala caste to ordain in their monastic fraternity.

9. For more about the process of recontextualisation, see Reed (1998).

10. The choice of creating the national dance from the regional form of the Kandyan territory was significant, as the Kandyan region (of the central mountainous hill country) "was the last religion of Lanka to be colonized by Europeans" and had "long been identified as the heartland of Sinhala Buddhist culture" (Reed 2010, 80–81). Although some parts of the Lanka had been successfully occupied and colonized by the Portuguese, Dutch, and British powers for over three hundred years, it was only with the fall of the Kandyan Kingdom in 1815 that the entire island was colonized by foreign powers. Similar to the domination of the Vellalars in the Jaffna Peninsula, Kandy was dominated by aristocratic, up-country Kandyan families who shaped the first postcolonial governments of Sri Lanka.

11. Navarathri is a nine-day Hindu festival that celebrates the Goddess in many of her forms.

Chapter 2

1. The progression of schooling and testing practices are based on the British model of public education. The General Certificate of Education Ordinary-Level examination is administered at grade 11, when students are fifteen to sixteen years old. Grade 13 is when students sit for the Advanced-Level examination, which is the university entrance exam in Sri Lanka.

2. The Sri Lankan Freedom Party (SLFP) under S. W. R. D. Bandaranaike introduced "Sinhala-Only" as a campaign strategy to amass votes. The result was electoral victory for the SLFP, and the Sinhala-Only Act was enacted after the election. The act was passed with the SLFP and the United National Party supporting it and with the Marxist-oriented Ceylon Equal Society Party, Communist Party (Ceylon), and the Tamil nationalist parties opposing it. Superficially targeting English-centric elitism, the policy had disturbing consequences for Tamils. During the early postcolonial period, English-educated Tamils were "overrepresented" in the state sector"; therefore the Sinhalese Only policy signaled a drastic shift in job opportunities in favor of Sinhalese speakers at the expense of Tamils (Bose 2007, 17). Thus, 1956 marked a year when Tamils were labeled a "minority," a community that had arrived in Sri Lanka only a millennium previously as a result of Tamil "invasions" from South India and as a "group that had been unduly privileged" under colonialism (18).

3. The association of Sinhala culture with Hindustani and North Indian classical music parallels the association of the Sinhala language with Aryan influence and the distance or division from the Tamil language associated with Dravidian culture. Several prominent Sinhala artists I met had trained at Shantiniketan in West Bengal, India, the town associated with the university established by Rabrindranath Tagore. The Tamil revival,

inspired in part by Arumuka Navalar's reforms in religion and language, also celebrated Carnatic music as Tamil culture (see Reed 2010; O'Shea 2016, 119).

4. Sanchari Bhava is a form of danced story-telling theater, which can incorporate improvisation to support the emotions of the song.

5. Kandyan dance is accepted as a national dance form. Reed's (2010) work illuminates how the ritual kohomba kankariya was "recontextualized" into the dance form "Kandyan dance," foremost a "traditional dance" of Sri Lanka. She maintains that by 1956, when Sri Lanka was experiencing a cultural renaissance that focused on resisting and rejecting remnants of British culture, dance became the promoted practice of Sri Lankan identity and, later on, Sinhala identity. She maintains that the dance form is divided along ethnic lines; however, bharata natyam is a popular dance form among the Sinhalese in both Buddhist and Christian communities (see chapter 1).

6. Tala is the term used for the rhythmic cycle in Indian classical music, comparable to meter in Western music.

7. Shloka is a metered and often rhymed poetic verse or phrase. Used in the Vedas, it has come to mean a proverb and a form of prayer.

8. *Namaskaram* is a movement done at the beginning and end of any bharata natyam dance session to pay respect to the guru, God, and the earth.

9. *Tatta adavu* is the first basic step in bharata natyam.

10. A traditional margam repertoire consists of about ten different types of dance compositions. The order and types of pieces presented has been attributed almost entirely to the Thanjavur quartet of the eighteenth century (see Meduri 1996).

11. Jatiswaram and *sabdam* are pieces incorporated in the traditional bharata natyam concert format or margam repertoire. Jatiswaram and *sabdam* are the second and third items learned by the bharata natyam student.

12. Abhinaya is the use of mime and expression used in bharata natyam to convey the meaning of a song or story (Lusti-Narasimhan 2002, 175).

13. Thus, although Kannangara believed "doing" was as important as "knowing," much of the syllabus was based on memorization and less on developing personal voice or creativity.

14. During my fieldwork I did not learn of Kandyan dance instruction offered in Tamil-medium schools. This association of Tamil with India fits well with concerns of Sri Lankan Tamils being associated with the Tamil Nadu sociopolitical community. Reed states, borrowing from Tambiah (1986), "The Sinhalas are often called a 'majority with a minority complex,' because of their anxiety about their status vis-à-vis the South Indian and Sri Lankan Tamil communities (1991, 190).

Chapter 3

1. *Ananda Nardana Ganapati* loosely translates as "beautiful, dancing, Ganapati." The composition *Ananda Nardana Ganapati* is in *ragam nattai*, *adi talam*, and the Sanskrit language. The composer is unknown.

2. The Fulbright Program is a program of international educational exchange for students, scholars, teachers, professionals, scientists, and artists, founded by U.S. senator

J. William Fulbright in 1946. Funded through the U.S. Congress, the U.S. Department of State's Bureau of Education and Cultural Affairs sponsors the Fulbright program. My own research trip was funded through the Fulbright-Hays Doctoral Dissertation Research Award, funded by the U.S. Department of Education. The Fulbright program has an office in Colombo and assists Sri Lankan and U.S. students and scholars.

3. The full line of this shloka is "Vakratunda Mahakaya Surya Koti Samaprabha; Neervigna Kurume Deva Sarva Karyeshu Sarvada." Aparna Chatterjee's (2005) provides this translation: "O Lord Ganesha possessing a large body and a curved trunk, with the brilliance of a million suns, make all my work free of obstacles always."

4. The demands of research articulate the construction of the practice not only of writing ethnography but of conducting such research. This demand binds the researcher to the process of participation, to investigating the activities to which doors are opened by informants and the community in which she finds herself. Several scholars have discussed the predicament in "writing up" fieldwork. Visweswaran approaches ethnography as a "fiction" (1994, 15). Visweswaran maintains that, although ethnography sets out to build a believable world, one that the reader accepts as factual, its approach is fundamentally incomplete, as it is detached from the world in which it reflects. In *Vulnerable Observer*, Behar asks the ethnographer to consider, "what happens within the observer" (1996, 6, 8–9). Both Visweswaran and Behar suggest an awareness of the construction of ethnography, a representation of events, people, and places. In response to this construction, they suggest a volunteering of the difficult moments, the documentation of "disjunctions" and "misunderstandings" (Visweswaran 1994) and an acknowledgment of "subjectivity" (Behar 1996, 7).

5. Through the lens of an "unruly-spectator," P. Srinivasan playfully and critically analyzes the saturation of "nationalist, Orientalist and patriarchal discourses" in bharata natyam (2009, 53). Building on the critical lens provided through participation (insider) and distance (outsider), this chapter similarly employs the lens of a dancer who is a spectator and ethnographer. Straddling an insider-outsider positionality, this lens is created through my embodied participation as a dancer of bharata natyam in Sri Lanka and abroad and a familiar spectator of the dance.

6. Krishnan's (2014) work on early Tamil cinema and dance shows that Bharati's work was already incorporated into early bharata natyam performances. The use of his work exemplifies the ways in which bharata natyam was malleable to address nationalist sentiments and social causes. Krishnan shows that early film was the means through which the dance creates itself as pan-Indian, detached from specific caste belonging and open to all, including the upper-caste and middle-class woman.

7. *Draupadhi* is another name for *Panchali*.

8. The exact date is unknown, but Bharati's *Panchali Sabatham* is estimated to have been written in the 1920s.

9. Pavala Vilzha performed the voice-over at the seventy-fifth anniversary celebration, Ladies' College, Colombo, May 11, 2007.

10. Music and lyrics for *Draupadhi Sabatham* were composed in Tamil by Kulendran (translation hers). I am integrating the lyrical descriptions in my ethnographic text.

11. In *nritta* mudras do not convey a specific meaning. A *mushti* mudra is a closed-fist hand gesture. Used here in the theatrical form of the dance, it demonstrates the grabbing and pulling of hair.

12. *Pataka* mudra is a stylized hand gesture, where the hand is held open and flat with the fingers aligned straight and tightly next to one another, and the thumb is held next to the palm with the knuckle bent. Here it is used to demonstrate a "pushing" action.

13. Om is considered a sacred sound in Hinduism. Stutley and Stutley describe it as "the root-syllable of origination and dissolution. . . . The past, present, and future are all included in this one sound, and all that exists beyond the three forms of time is also implied in it" (1977, 213).

14. Several scholars criticize the portrayal of women as victims of conflict because it undermines their creative resistance and omits "how long-term social upheaval might have also transformed women's often subordinate gender roles" (Rajasingham-Senanayake 1999, 139–40).

15. Yogendran, in discussion with the author, March 6, 2007.

16. Premawathie Manamperi (1949–71) was a beauty queen from Kataragama, in the south of Sri Lanka, who was beaten and murdered as the Sri Lankan army forcefully tried to bring the city, a hotbed of JVP insurgent activity, under control. In April 1971 the two volunteer members of the Sri Lankan army took control of several young women, including Premawathie. They interrogated Premawathie about her involvement with the insurgents. When they received no information from her, they made her strip and walk naked through the town. They then shot her and buried her alive, returning to finally kill her.

17. Yogendran's reference to Jaffna places it as a site of Tamil origin and a historical source of culture. She questions the integrity of rituals observed in the cosmopolitan and ethnically diverse city of Colombo.

18. *Nattuvangam* is a rhythmic instrument played in bharata natyam performances. It consists of two small cymbals that fit in the hand: one is iron, and the other is brass. Dissociated from the *nattuvanar*, which was of an exclusive caste (associated with the devadasi caste), the *nattuvangam* is now played by artists trained to perform the instrument. The *nattuvangam* artists also utter rhythmic syllables that accompany the performance.

19. *Buddham saranam gacchami, dhammam saranam gacchami, sangham saranam gacchami* translates as "I go to the Buddha for refuge; I go to the Dhamma for refuge; I go to the *sangha* for refuge." The invocation marks a commitment to taking Buddha's teaching as a guide to one's life. *Om shanti shanti shanti* translates as "Om, peace, peace, peace."

20. *Anjali* mudra is a double-handed gesture, where the palms of the hands press against each other; it is often used for greeting and prayer.

21. *Jugalbandi* is a duet performance in Hindustani, or both Carnatic and Hindustani, classical music that features two solo musicians on equal footing. *Jugalbandis* of Hindustani and Carnatic styles typically feature artists from each tradition collaborating and presenting a piece common to both traditions.

22. The Cease-Fire Agreement between the government of Sri Lanka and the LTTE was enacted on February 23, 2002, temporarily ending nineteen years of civil conflict.

Chapter 4

1. We did not refer to the piece as *Title Dance* but instead referred to it as the *Shakthi Superstar* piece. For the purpose of clarity, I refer to the piece as *Title Dance*.

2. Kollywood is a colloquial term used to describe Tamil cinema, a portmanteau of the Kodambakkam neighborhood of Chennai, Tamil Nadu, India, where the films are produced and Hollywood, the famous neighborhood in Los Angeles known for U.S. cinema. Bollywood, the largest film industry in India, is a similar portmanteau named after Mumbai, Maharashtra, India (which is also known as Bombay, its official name until 1995) and Hollywood.

3. These inconveniences are arguably different based on ethnic identity as well. Winslow and Woost write,

> For Tamil Sri Lankans, such as those on their way to work each morning, the implications were more ominous. They feared and worried over checkpoints, where they were far more likely than either foreigners or Sinhalese residents to be pulled over, taken from a bus, taxi, or bicycle to be interrogated, and even taken away and detained. Perhaps it resulted only in being late for work or some appointment, but even that could be a significant cost. Both Sinhala and Tamil residents suggested to us that employers were reluctant to hire Tamils because they too often were delayed at checkpoints. It was not that Tamils were unreliable; it was simply that they experienced the "normalization" of security in a particularly costly fashion. (2004, 12)

4. *Shakthi Superstar* features a group of contestants, chosen from various parts of the country, who sing a variety of popular songs and are then evaluated by a panel of judges. Unlike *American Idol*, for instance, in *Shakthi Superstar*, it is only in the final round that the viewers select the winner.

5. Yamini's work utilizes footwork in bharata natyam adavus but also incorporates quick, lightly stepped movements that are not incorporated in the canon of the bharata natyam technique. She does, however, incorporate mudras in her work and arm positions that are in adavus, but these too are "delicate" in their appearance, as the elbows are more rounded and less angular.

6. Frequently, we would describe an adherence to the traditional repertoire and vocabulary of bharata natyam as "heavy" or "classical," which is why Padmini's use of "light" to describe a departure from bharata natyam is understood by all of us. Light is a descriptor often used in music, for example, light rock.

7. Vyjayanthimala Bali, as Krishnan (2014) illuminates, is a figure that, through cinema, furthered the establishment of bharata natyam as a classical form through her upper-caste body and her dancing. The dismissal of the dancing woman that is taking place through these debates in creating *Title Dance* demonstrate strong currents of respectability that continue the construction between the popular and classical, the cinematic and art. The association of Hindu nymphs with the dance on film, here, evoke the lasting imagery and interweaving threads of Orientalism and nationalism—the spiritual—and the nation that took place with the cinematic dance in the mid-twentieth century.

8. During the conversation the term *busque* was used, which I later learned is a fifteenth-century term for a piece of a women's corset. I am not sure what the official term for this part of the bharata natyam costume is. I have heard it referred to as the "seat" as well.

9. *Akka* means "older sister" in Tamil and is often used as a term of respect for any relatively older female.

10. *Title Dance* was subject to market forces, and, in the end, the several degrees of authority (from dancer to season-finale producer) were subject to those forces. Limón discusses "the profitable political economy of the dance, with its marked tendency to treat the dancers as commodities and consumers" (1994, 164).

11. My status as an American and outsider was not always effaced. It was definitely recognized during tech rehearsal, when there was an argument over the expenses we bore to participate in the show. Padmini gave us each two thousand rupees (approx. US$20 at the time). I offered to pay dinner that night to a few friends who mentioned their financial hardship. I was labeled a "rich American."

12. For a longer discussion on "barriers of accommodation," see chapter 1.

Conclusion

1. *Kanchipuram* is a specific type of silk sari made in the Kanchipuram region of Tamil Nadu. The sari style is distinct through its use of wide contrast borders and the designs through the weaving of *zari*, or gold thread. *Kanchipuram* is typically used in the creation of bharata natyam costumes. Dancers also use polyester-silk blends woven in the *kanchipuram* style. *Katakamukha* mudra means "opening in a bracelet" and is a hand gesture where the index finger, middle finger, and the thumb are brought to touch, while the ring and little finger are stretched way from the palm.

2. The Tamil Makkal Viduthalai Pulikal was formed in 2004 by Muralitharan, known as Colonel Karuna, who was the LTTE head of the Eastern Province for more than twenty years. Since the end of the war, Karuna served as a minister of Parliament (2008–15) in the Rajapaksa government. In 2017 he launched a new political party, the Tamil United Freedom Party (Press Trust of India 2017).

3. The civil conflict has created a large diasporic Sri Lankan community, numbering some eight hundred thousand people. Thiranagama (2011) also discusses a presence of "shadow diaspora" in Colombo, composed of those waiting for migration papers. Tamils fleeing the war were accepted as refugees in Canada and parts of Europe, forming substantial communities there. Diasporic politics in terms of support for the Tigers, however, has often been discordant with Sri Lanka–based Tamil communities (Orjuela and Sriskandarajah 2008).

4. The Indian High Commission in Sri Lanka oversees the Indian Cultural Centre, which functions through the patronage of the embassy of India "for the purpose of advancement of sport, social and cultural activities of the Indian community in Colombo." The center includes in its initiatives the marking of "important festivals in Buddhist practice and Lord Buddha's life," the organizing of events to "honor various Indian artists and philosophers," and the funding of "study abroad exchanges focusing on music and dance" (Indian High Commission 2013).

5. According to Destradi, India supported the Sri Lankan government's military offensive against the Tigers and initially opposed the investigation of war crimes by the United Nations Human Rights Council (UNHRC) when the war ended (2012, 596).

6. Since the middle of the first decade of the 2000s, as the (Norway-brokered) Cease-Fire Agreement crumbled and final phase of the war began, China has become a significant donor and ally to the Sri Lankan state. The relationship between the two states is marked by increased economic cooperation, the construction of huge infrastructure projects in Sri Lanka, and, during the war, China's provisions of weapons to the Sri Lankan army. The influence of the country in Sri Lanka has shaken certain powers in South Asia, specifically India, and impacted India's policy shift on Sri Lankan affairs (Uyangoda 2008).

7. Padmini (pseudonym), pers. comm. with the author, September 12, 2012, Colombo, Sri Lanka.

8. These inconveniences are arguably different based on ethnic identity as well. Winslow and Woost write, "For Tamil Sri Lankans, such as those on their way to work each morning, the implications were more ominous. They feared and worried over checkpoints, where they were far more likely than either foreigners or Sinhalese residents to be pulled over, taken from a bus, taxi, or bicycle to be interrogated, and even taken away and detained" (2004, 12).

Bibliography

Allen, Matthew Harp. 1997. "Rewriting the Script for South Indian Dance." *Drama Review: A Journal of Performance Studies* 41 (3): 63–100.

Appadurai, Arjun. 1996. *Modernity at Large: Cultural Dimensions of Globalization.* Minneapolis: University of Minnesota Press.

Arasaratnam, Sinnappah. 1997. "Nationalism in Sri Lanka and the Tamils." In Roberts 1997, 295–314.

"Art Clear of Modern Trends." n.d. Scrapbook of Daya Mahinda. Circa 1930–60. Colombo.

Arundale, Rukmini Devi. 2003. *Some Selected Speeches and Writings of Rukmini Devi Arundale* 2 vols. Chennai: Kalakshetra Foundation.

Balendra, W. n.d. "How National Dances Became Fashionable." N.p.

Bandara, H. H. 1972. *Cultural Policy in Sri Lanka.* Paris: United Nations Educational, Scientific, and Cultural Organization.

Bartholomeusz, Tessa J. 1994. *Women under the Bo Tree: Buddhist Nuns in Sri Lanka.* London: Cambridge University Press.

Baskaran, S. Theodore. 1991. "Music for the Masses: Film Songs of Tamil Nadu." *Economic and Political Weekly* 26 (11–12): 755–58.

Beehner, Lionel. 2010. "The 31 Places to Go in 2010." *New York Times*, January 10, 2010.

Behar, Ruth. 1996. *The Vulnerable Observer: Anthropology That Breaks Your Heart.* Boston: Beacon.

Bhabha, Homi K. 1992. "Freedom's Basis in the Indeterminate." *October* 61:46–57.

———. 1994. *The Location of Culture.* New York: Routledge.

Bharati, Subramania. 1977. *Poems of Subramania Bharati.* Translated by Prema Nandakumar Prema. New Delhi: Sahitya Akademi.

———. 1979. *Selected Poems of Subramania Bharati.* Translated by Krishna Srinivas. Madras: Poet Press.

———. 1990. *Kavithaihal.* Chennai: Sri Inthu.

Bose, Sumantra. 2007. *Contested Lands: Israel-Palestine, Kashmir, Bosnia, Cyprus, and Sri Lanka.* Cambridge, MA: Harvard University Press.

"A Brief History of the JVP (Peoples Liberation Front) Sri Lanka." 1999. *People's Liberation Front: JVP Sri Lanka.* Accessed April 18 2019. www.jvpsrilanka.com /english/about-us/brief-history/.

Bureau of the Commissioner General of Rehabilitation. 2011. "Introduction." Accessed April 26, 2019. bcgr.gov.lk/history.php.

Butler, Judith, and Gayatri Chakravorty Spivak. 2007. *Who Sings the Nation-State?* London: Seagull Books.

"The Ceylon Causerie." 1951. N.p.

Chakravorty, Pallabi. 2006. "Dancing into Modernity: Multiple Narratives of India's Kathak Dance." *Dance Research Journal* 38 (1–2): 115–36.

Chatterjee, Aparna. 2005. "Shree Geneshaya Namah." *Boloji.com*. December 18, 2005. www.boloji.com/index.cfm?md=Content&sd=Articles&ArticleID=1611.

Chatterjee, Partha. 1990. "The Nationalist Resolution of the Women's Question." In *Recasting Women: Essays in Indian Colonial History*, edited by Kumkum Sangari and Sudesh Vaid, 233–53. New Brunswick: Rutgers University Press.

Cole, Catherine. 2007. "Performance, Transitional Justice, and the Law: South Africa's Truth and Reconciliation" *Theatre Journal* 59 (2): 167–87.

Cumming-Bruce, Nick. 2012. "In Resolution, U.N. Council Presses Sri Lanka on Civilian Deaths." *New York Times*, March 23, 2012.

Daniel, Smriti. 2017. "Sri Lanka is Creating a New Constitution and the People Have Spoken—More Than 7,000 of Them." *Scroll*, January 9, 2017. https://scroll.in /article/826105/sri-lanka-is-the-process-of-creating-a-new-constitution-and-the -people-have-spoken.

Das, Veena, and Arthur Kleinman. 2000. Introduction to *Violence and Subjectivity*, edited by Veena Das, Arthur Kleinman, Mamphela Ramphele, and Pamela Reynolds, 1–18. Berkeley: University of California Press.

David, Ann. 2008. "Local Diasporas/Global Trajectories: New Aspects of Religious 'Performance' in British Tamil Hindu Practice." *Performance Research* 13 (3): 89–99.

De Alwis, Malathi. 1997. "The Production and Embodiment of 'Respectability': Gendered Demeanours in Colonial Ceylon." In Roberts 1997, 105–43.

———. 2002. "The Changing Role of Women in Sri Lankan Society." *Social Research* 69 (3): 675–91.

———. 2009. "Interrogating the 'Political': Feminist Peace Activism in Sri Lanka." *Feminist Review* 91:81–93.

De Mel, Neloufer. 2001. *Women and the Nation's Narrative: Gender and Nationalism in Twentieth Century Sri Lanka*. New Delhi: Kali for Women.

———. 2003. "Agent or Victim? The Sri Lankan Woman Militant in the Interregnum." In *Feminists under Fire: Exchanges across War Zones*, edited by Wenona Giles, Malathi de Alwis, Edith Klein, and Neluka Silva, 55–74. Toronto: Between the Lines.

———. 2009. "Gendering the New Security Paradigm in Sri Lanka." *IDS Bulletin* 40 (2): 36–43.

Desai, Radhika. 2008. "Introduction: Nationalisms and Their Understandings in Historical Perspective." *Third World Quarterly* 29 (3): 397–428.

De Silva, Chandra Richard, and Daya de Silva. 1990. *Education in Sri Lanka, 1948–1988*. New Delhi: Navrang.

Destradi, Sandra. 2012. "India and Sri Lanka's Civil War." *Asian Survey* 52 (3): 595–616.

DeVotta, Neil. 2000. "Control Democracy, Institutional Decay, and the Quest for Eelam: Explaining Ethnic Conflict in Sri Lanka." *Pacific Affairs* 73 (1): 55–76.

———. 2004. *Blowback: Linguistic Nationalism, Institutional Decay, and Ethnic Conflict in Sri Lanka*. Stanford, CA: Stanford University Press.

———. 2009 "The Liberation Tigers of Tamil Eelam and the Lost Quest for Separatism in Sri Lanka." *Asian Survey* 49 (6): 1021–51.

Dhand, Arti. 2004. "The Subversive Nature of Virtue in the Mahābhārata: A Tale about

Women, Smelly Ascetics, and God." *Journal of the American Academy of Religion* 72 (1): 33–58.

Duggan, Lisa. 2003. *Twilight of Equality: Neoliberalism, Cultural Politics, and the Attack on Democracy*. Boston: Beacon.

Elder, James. 2009. "Bring Back the Child: UNICEF and Sri Lanka Launch Media Campaign on Child Soldiers." *UNICEF*. February 26, 2009. www.unicef.org/infoby country/sri_lanka_48286.html.

Engquist, Olle, Lars Jivén, and Kjell Nyström. 1981. *Education and Training in Sri Lanka: A Sector Analysis*. N.p.: Swedish International Development Agency.

Erdman, Joan. 1987. "Performance as Translation: Uday Shankar in the West." *Drama Review: A Journal of Performance Studies* 31 (1): 64–88.

Ethirajan, Anbarasan. 2009. "How Sri Lanka's Military Won." *BBC News*. May 22, 2009. http://news.bbc. co.uk/2/hi/8063409.stm.

Fernando, Laksiri. 2016. "Jaffna University Sinhala-Tamil Student Conflict Was Insane." *Colombo Telegraph*, July 22, 2016. www.colombotelegraph.com/index.php/jaffna -university-sinhala-tamil-student-conflict-was-insane/.

"Finalists in the Dance Festival." 1950. *Times of Ceylon*, November 8, 1950.

Gamage, Daya. 2012. "U.N.—Declaring Dereliction of Its Duty in Sri Lanka's Separatist War—Makes Case for 'Global Security' in 'Tell All' Report." *Asian Tribune News*. November 18, 2012. http://asiantribune.com/news/2012/11/17/un-declaring -dereliction-its-duty-sri-lankas-separatist-war-makes-case-global-scruti.

Gilroy, Paul. 1993. *The Black Atlantic: Modernity and Double Consciousness*. Cambridge, MA: Harvard University Press.

Goodhand, Jonathan. 2012. "Sri Lanka in 2011 Consolidation and Militarization of the Post-War Regime." *Asian Survey* 52 (1): 130–37.

Guilmoto, Christophe Z. 1993. "The Tamil Migration Cycle, 1830–1950." *Economic and Political Weekly* 28 (3–4): 111–20.

Gunawardena, Ranaweera Appuhamilage Leslie Herbert. 1990. *The People of the Lion: The Sinhala Identity and Ideology in History and Historiography*, edited by Jonathan Spencer, 45–86. New York: Routledge.

Herr, Ranjoo Seodu. 2003. "The Possibility of Nationalist Feminism." *Hypatia* 16 (3): 135–60.

Hiltebeitel, Alfred. 1981. "Draupadi's Hair" *Purusartha* 5:179–214.

hooks, bell. 2000. *Feminist Theory: From Margin to Center*. New York: South End.

———. 2008. "Talking Back." 1984. In *Women Images and Realities: A Multicultural Anthology*, 4th ed., edited by Amy Kesselman, Lily D. McNair, and Nany Schniedewind, 15–18. Boston: McGraw-Hill.

Indian High Commission. 2013. "About Us." December 13, 2013. www.hcicolombo.org /index.php?option=com_pages&id=7.

"Indigenous Dancing" n.d. Scrapbook of Daya Mahinda. Circa 1930–60. Colombo.

Iyer, E. Krishna. 1950. "Dancing Should Be Part of School Education." *Ceylon Observer*, November 26, 1950.

———. n.d. "Indian Dance Art in Ceylon." Scrapbook of Daya Mahinda. Circa 1930–60. Colombo.

Jackson, Naomi M., and Toni Shapiro-Phim, eds. 2008. *Dance, Human Rights, and Social Justice: Dignity in Motion*. Plymouth, UK: Scarecrow.

Jayawardena, Kumari, and Malathi de Alwis. 1996. *Embodied Violence: Communalising Women's Sexuality in South Asia*. London: Zed Books.

Jeganathan, Pradeep. 2003. "In the Shadow of a Riot: 1983 and After." *Nethra* 6 (1–2): 139–59.

Kadirgamar, Ahilan. 2010. "Classes, States and the Politics of the Tamil Diaspora." *Economic and Political Weekly* 45 (31): 23–26.

———. 2015. "Neoliberal State, Rural Dispossession and Struggles for Education." In *Neoliberalism, Critical Pedagogy and Education*, edited by Ravi Kumar, 135–47. New York: Taylor and Francis.

———. 2017. "The Failure of Post-War Reconstruction in Jaffna, Sri Lanka: Indebtedness, Caste Exclusion and the Search for Alternatives." PhD diss., City University New York.

Kailasapathy, Kanagasabapathy. "The Tamil Purist Movement: A Re-evaluation." *Social Scientist* 7 (10): 23–51.

"Kalalayathin Aimbathandu Varalaaru." 1998. In *Golden Anniversary Souvenir Booklet*. Colombo: Kalalaya School of Music and Dance.

Kersenboom-Story, Saskia. 1987. *Nityasumangali: Devadasi Tradition in South India*. Delhi: Motilal Banarsidass.

Khubchandani, Kareem. 2016. "Snakes on the Dance Floor: Bollywood, Gesture, and Gender." *Velvet Light Trap* 77:69–95.

Kondo, Dorinne K. 1990. *Crafting Selves: Power, Gender, and Discourses of Identity in a Japanese Workplace*. Chicago: University of Chicago Press.

Krishnan, Hari. 2014. "Celluloid Classicism: Intertwined Histories of the South Indian Dance Revival and Early South Indian Cinema" Wesleyan University. September 24, 2014. https://video.wesleyan.edu/videos/video/3832198308001.

Kulendran, Gnana. 2007. "Panchali Sabatham." *Tamil Maanavar Sangam*. Ladies College, Colombo.

Lakshmi, C. S. 1999. "Bodies Called Women: Some Thoughts on Gender, Ethnicity and Nation." In Thiruchandran 1999, 53–88.

Lefebvre, Henri. 1991. *The Production of Space*. Translated by Donald Nicholson-Smith. Hoboken: Wiley-Blackwell.

Limón, José Eduardo. 1994. *Dancing with the Devil: Society and Cultural Poetics in Mexican-American South Texas*. Madison: University of Wisconsin Press.

Little, David. 1994. *Sri Lanka: The Invention of Enmity*. Washington, DC: United States Institute of Peace Press.

Lowe, Lisa. 1996. *Immigrant Acts: On Asian American Cultural Politics*. Durham: Duke University Press.

Lusti-Narasimhan, Manjula. 2002. *Bharatanatyam*. New Delhi: Bookwise.

McGilvray, Dennis. 1998. "Arabs, Moors and Muslims: Sri Lankan Muslim Ethnicity in Regional Perspective." *Contributions to Indian Sociology* 32 (2): 433–83.

———. 2008. *Crucible of Conflict: Tamil and Muslim Society on the East Coast of Sri Lanka*. Durham: Duke University Press.

Meduri, Avanthi. 1996. "Nation, Woman, Representation: The Sutured History of the Devadasi and Her Dance." PhD diss., New York University.

———. 2001. "Bharata Natyam: What Are You?" In *Moving History, Dancing Culture*, edited by Ann Daly and Ann Cooper Albright, 103–12. Middletown, CT: Wesleyan University Press.

Ministry of Education and Ministry of Higher Education. 1986. *Development of Education, 1984–1986*. Sri Jayawardhanepura: Sri Lanka Ministry of Education.

Morris, Gay, and Jens Giersdorf, eds. 2016. *Choreographies of 21st Century Wars*. New York: Oxford University Press.

Nessman, Ravi. 2008. "Sri Lanka Tamils Live in Fear, and Resignation, of Security Forces." *New York Times*, September 1, 2008.

Nissan, Elizabeth, and Roderick L. Stirrat. 1990. "The Generation of Communal Identities." In Spencer 1990, 19–44.

Ong, Aihwa. 2007. "Neoliberalism as a Mobile Technology" *Transactions of the Institute of British Geographers*, n.s., 32 (1): 3–8.

"On Versions of the Ramayana and Mahabharata in South-East Asia." 2004. *Sunday Vijay Times* (Bangalore), May 30, 2004. *Kauntext*. https://raahi.wordpress.com/tag/art/.

"Oriental Dance-Drama." 1950. *Daily News*, October 9, 1950.

Orjuela, Camilla, and Dhananjayan Sriskandarajah. 2008. "The Sri Lankan Tamil Diaspora: Warmongers or Peace-Builders?" In *Transnational South Asians: The Making of Neo-diaspora*, edited by Susan Koshy and Rajagopalan Radhakrishnan, 325–41. Oxford: Oxford University Press.

O'Shea, Janet. 2007. *At Home in the World: Bharata Natyam on the Global Stage*. Middletown, CT: Wesleyan University Press.

———. 2016. "From Temple to Battlefield." In Morris and Giersdorf 2016, 111–32.

Peiris, Roshan. 1983. "Kamala Johnpillai: 'My Humble Salutations at Your Feet.'" *Sunday Observer* (Colombo), July 24, 1983.

Perera, Lal, Swarna Wijetunge, and A. S. Balasooriya. 2004. "Education Reform and Political Violence in Sri Lanka." In Tawil and Harley 2004, 375–415.

Perera, Sulakshani, 2012. "Sri Lanka's Displacement Chapter Nears End with Closure of Menik Farm." *UNHCR*, September 27, 2012. www.unhcr.org/news/latest/2012/9/506443d89/sri-lankas-displacement-chapter-nears-end-closure-menik-farm.html.

Pfaffenberger, Bryan. 1979. "Kataragama Pilgrimage: Hindu-Buddhist Interaction and Its Significance in Sri-Lanka's Poly-ethnic Social System." *Journal of Asian Studies* 38 (2): 253–70.

———. 1981. "The Cultural Dimension of Tamil Separatism in Sri Lanka." *Asian Survey* 21 (11): 1145–57.

———. 1994. "Introduction: The Sri Lankan Tamils." In *The Sri Lankan Tamils: Ethnicity and Identity*, edited by Chelvadurai Manogaran and Bryan Pfaffenberger, 1–27. Boulder: Westview.

Phelan, Peggy. 1993. *Unmarked*. New York: Routledge.

"The President Reminisces." 2000. In *Mangaiyar Malar, 1930–1998*, 17–32. Colombo: Saiva Mangaiyar Kalaham.

Press Trust of India. 2013. "LTTE Chief Prabhakaran's Son's Killing: It's Lies and Half

Truths, Says Sri Lanka." *India Today*, February 19, 2013. www.indiatoday.in/world
/story/ltte-prabhakaran-son-balachandran-killing-sri-lanka-defends-154457-2013
-02-19 Accessed April 22, 2019.

———. 2017. "Rebel LTTE Leader Karuna Forms Political Party." *Hindu*, February 12,
2017. www.thehindu.com/news/international/Rebel-LTTE-leader-Karuna-forms
-political-party/article17291844.ece.

Prins, Steven. 2011. "A National Treasure." *Sunday Times* (Colombo), August 21, 2011.
www.sundaytimes.lk/110821/Plus/plus_01.5.html.

Prothero, Stephen. 1995. "Henry Steel Olcott and 'Protestant Buddhism.'" *Journal of the
American Academy of Religion* 63 (2): 281–302.

Rajasingham-Senanayake, Darini. 1999. "Post Victimisation: Cultural Transformation
and Women's Empowerment in War and Displacement." In Thiruchandran 1999,
136–51.

———. 2005. "Neoliberalism and the Structural Adjustment of the Sociological
Imagination: Development Discourse and the Triumph of Homo Oeconomicus."
Sociological Bulletin 54 (3): 551–73.

Ramnarayan, Gowri. 1984. "Rukmini Devi: A Quest for Beauty." *Sruti* 8 (June 1984):
17–30.

Reed, Susan A. 1991. "The Transformation of Ritual and Dance in Sri Lanka: Kohomba
Kankariya and the Kandyan Dance." PhD diss., Brown University.

———. 1998. "The Politics and Poetics of Dance." *Annual Review of Anthropology* 27:
503–32.

———. 2010. *Dance and the Nation: Performance, Ritual, and Politics in Sri Lanka.*
Madison: University of Wisconsin Press.

"Rhythm of Life." n.d. Scrapbook of Daya Mahinda. Circa 1930–60. Colombo.

Roberts, Michael. 1978. "Ethnic Conflict in Sri Lanka and Sinhalese Perspectives:
Barriers to Accommodation." *Modern Asian Studies* 12 (3): 353–76.

———, ed. 1997. *Sri Lanka: Collective Identities Revisited.* Vol. 1. Colombo: Marga
Institute.

Rogers, John. 1990. "Historical Images in the British Period." In Spencer 1990, 205–25.

———. 1994. "Post-Orientalism and the Interpretation of Premodern and Modern
Political Identities: The Case of Sri Lanka." *Journal of Asian Studies* 53 (1): 10–23.

Ruwanpura, Kanchana N. 2008. "The Gender and Spatial Politics of NGOs: Spaces
of Subversion, Sites of Reinforcement." In *Constellations of Violence: Feminist
Interventions in South Asia*, edited by Radhika Coomaraswamy and Nimanth Perera-
Rajasingham, 93–120. New Delhi: Women Unlimited.

Said, Edward. 1978. *Orientalism.* New York: Pantheon Books.

"Saiva Mangaiyar Vidyalayam: Hindu Ladies College." 1998. In *Mangaiyar Malar, 1930–
1998*, 24–25. Colombo: Saiva Mangaiyar Kalaham.

Savigliano, Marta. 1995. *Tango and the Political Economy of Passion.* Boulder: Westview.

Schrijvers, Joke. 1999. "Constructing 'Womanhood,' 'Tamilness,' and 'The Refugee':
Internal Refugees in Sri Lanka." In Thiruchandran 1999, 169–201.

Scott, Anna Beatrice. 1997. "Spectacle and Dancing Bodies That Matter: Or, If It Don't

Fit, Don't Force It." In *Meaning in Motion: New Cultural Studies of Dance*, edited by
Jane Desmond, 259–68. Durham: Duke University Press.

Selvadurai, Shyam. 1998. *Cinnamon Gardens*. New York: Hyperion.

Sengupta, Somini. 2009. "Sri Lanka Orders Halt to Fighting Circled Rebels." *New York
Times*, April 13, 2009.

Silva, Neluka. 2002. *The Hybrid Island: Culture Crossings and the Invention of Identity in Sri
Lanka*. London: Zed Books.

Soneji, Davesh. 2010. "Śiva's Courtesans: Religion, Rhetoric, and Self-Representation
in Early Twentieth-Century Writing by Devadāsīs." *International Journal of Hindu
Studies* 14 (1): 31–70.

———. 2012. *Unfinished Gestures: Devadasis, Memory and Modernity in South India*.
Chicago: University of Chicago Press.

Spencer, Jonathan. 1990. *Sri Lanka: History and the Roots of Conflict*. New York:
Routledge.

———. 2008. "A Nationalism without Politics? The Illiberal Consequences of Liberal
Institutions in Sri Lanka." *Third World Quarterly* 29 (3): 611–29.

Spivak, Gayatri Chakravorty. 1993. *Outside in the Teaching Machine*. New York: Routledge.

"Sri Lankan Rebels Launch Air Raid." 2007. *BBC News*, March 26, 2007. http://news.bbc
.co.uk/2/hi/south_asia/6494121.stm.

"Sri Lanka Says Leader of Rebels Has Died." 2009. *New York Times*, May 19, 2009.

Sri Lanka Special Committee on Education. 1943. *Ceylon Sessional Papers, 1943*. Colombo:
Ceylon Government Press.

Srinivasan, Amrit. 1985. "Reform and Revival: The Devadasi and Her Dance." *Economic
and Political Weekly* 20 (44): 1869–76.

Srinivasan, Priya. 2009. "A 'Material'-ist Reading of the Bharata Natyam Dancing Body:
The Possibility of the 'Unruly Spectator.'" In *Worlding Dance*, edited by Susan Foster.
New York: Palgrave, 2009.

———. 2011. *Sweating Saris: Indian Dance as Transnational Labor*. Philadelphia: Temple
University Press.

Stutley, Margaret, and James Stutley. 1997. *A Dictionary of Hinduism: Its Mythology,
Folklore and Development, 1500 B.C.–A.D. 1500*. London: Routledge and Kegan Paul.

Sullivan, Bruce. 2011. "The 'Mahābhārata': Perspectives on Its Ends and Endings."
International Journal of Hindu Studies 15 (1): 1–7.

Swarr, Amanda Lock, and Richa Nagar, eds. 2010. *Critical Transnational Feminist Praxis*.
Albany: State University of New York Press.

Tambiah, Stanley J. 1986. *Sri Lanka: Ethnic Fratricide and the Dismantling of Democracy*.
Chicago: University of Chicago Press.

———. 1992. *Buddhism Betrayed? Religion, Politics, and Violence in Sri Lanka*. Chicago:
University of Chicago Press.

Tawil, Sobhi, and Alexandra Harley. 2004. *Education Conflict and Social Cohesion*. Paris:
International Bureau of Education, UNESCO.

Taylor, Diana. 2003. *The Archive and Repertoire: Performing Cultural Memory in the
Americas*. Durham: Duke University Press.

Taylor, Julie. 1998. *Paper Tangos*. Durham: Duke University Press.

Tenekoon, Serena. 1990. "Newspaper Nationalism: Sinhala Identity as Historical Discourse." In Spencer 1990, 205–25.

Thapar, Romila. 2009. "War in the 'Mahabharata'" *PMLA* 124 (5): 1830–33.

Thiranagama, Sharika. 2011. *In My Mother's House: Civil War in Sri Lanka*. Philadelphia: University of Pennsylvania Press.

Thiruchandran, Selvy. 1998. *The Spectrum of Femininity: A Process of Deconstruction*. Delhi: Vikas.

————, ed. 1999. *Women, Nation and Narration: Collective Images and Multiple Identities*. Delhi: Vikas.

"Tough Action Eases Rioting." *Daily News*, July 27, 1983, 1.

"US Calls for Sri Lanka Ceasefire." 2009. *BBC News*. April 25, 2009. http://news.bbc .co.uk/2/hi/south_asia/8017843.stm.

Uyangoda, Jeyadeva. 2008. *The Way We Are: Politics of Sri Lanka, 2007–2008*. Colombo: Social Scientists' Research Association.

————. 2010. "Sri Lanka in 2009: From Civil War to Political Uncertainties." *Asian Survey* 50 (1): 104–11.

Uyangoda, Jeyadeva, and Kumari Jayawardena. 2010. "Sri Lanka's Past Year." *Polity* 5 (5): 2–3.

Visweswaran, Kamala. 1994. *Fictions of Feminist Ethnography*. Minneapolis: University of Minnesota Press.

Wanasinghe, Jayampati. 1988. "A Study of the Emergence of the Free Education Scheme in Sri Lanka and a Critical Analysis of Policies Formulated for Its Survival." *International Journal of Educational Development* 8 (2): 99–108.

Wayland, Sarah. 2004. "Ethnonationalist Networks and Transnational Opportunities: The Sri Lankan Tamil Diaspora." *Review of International Studies* 30 (3): 405–26.

Wickremasinghe, Nira. 2007. "Multiculturalism: A View from Sri Lanka." *Open Democracy*. May 30, 2007. www.opendemocracy.net/colonial_multiculturalism.jsp.

Williams, Raymond. 1995. *The Sociology of Culture*. Chicago: University of Chicago Press.

Wilson, A. Jeyaratnam. 1988. *The Break-Up of Sri Lanka: The Sinhalese-Tamil Conflict*. London: Hurst.

————. 2000. *Sri Lankan Tamil Nationalism: Its Origins and Development in the Nineteenth and Twentieth Centuries*. London: Hurst.

Wilson, Richard A. 2001. *The Politics of Truth and Reconciliation in South Africa: Legitimizing the Post-Apartheid State*. Cambridge: Cambridge University Press.

Winslow, Deborah, and Michael D. Woost. 2004. "Articulations of Economy and Ethnic Conflict in Sri Lanka." In *Economy, Culture, and Civil War in Sri Lanka*, edited by Deborah Winslow and Michael D. Woost, 1–28. Bloomington: Indiana University Press.

Yuval-Davis, Nira, and Marcel Stoetzler. 2002. "Imagined Boundaries and Borders: A Gendered Gaze." *European Journal of Women's Studies* 9 (3): 329–44.

Zolberg, Aristide R., Astri Suhrke, and Sergio Aguayo. 1989. *Escape from Violence: Conflict and the Refugee Crisis in the Developing World*. New York: Oxford University Press.

Index

Note: Page numbers with "n" or "nn" indicate material located in endnotes.

classical dance, 38, 86–87, 111–15, 116, 118, 133, 149n7

Cole, Catherine, 138–39

collective social reform, 26

Colombo, Sri Lanka: bharata natyam, 13, 26–29, 30, 45, 71–72; Cinnamon Gardens, 49, 81, 92, 144n2; civil war, 7–8, 82, 136; dance teachers, 66–67, 71–74; and identity, 10–11; Jegnathan on, 79; militarization, 2, 49, 96–97, 102; multiculturalism, 99–100; Padmini's productions in, 133–34; riots, 47–49; segregation, 100–101; shadow diaspora, 150n3; Tamilness, 65, 78, 89

Colombo Telegraph (newspaper), 139

colonialism: British, 4–5, 27–28, 32–33, 40, 42, 55–56; education, 52–53, 55–56; ethnic identity, 4–5; and gender, 30, 32–33; and the Other, 45–46; repertoire, 101; settler, 140

Committee of Inquiry into the Teaching of Art, Music and Dance, 71

common core curriculum, 52, 70–71

communalism, 5, 27, 53, 143–44n11

community-based organizations (CBOs), 136

competition model, 57

Coomaraswamy, Ananada, 53

costuming, 116–18, 121, 123, 150n8

court-style dances, 28

creativity, 65, 69

cultural, 53–55, 74–75, 136

Cultural Policy in Sri Lanka (Bandera), 52

culture: British, 27; differences, 32–33, 100; education, 56; identification, 4; and identity, 50–51, 62; Indian, 39, 140; indigenous, 59–60; knowledge and understanding, 65; legacy, 135; loss, 50–51; memory, 126; multiculturalism, 50–51, 58, 75, 94, 97–100, 102, 104–5; nationalism, 7, 53–55, 74–75, 136; nation building, 52–55, 59; one culture concept, 53; popular, 108, 112, 115, 121; practices, 2, 62; production, 8–9; re-

covery and revival, 52–53; signifiers, 105; Sinhala, 100, 145n3; sociology of, 14; Sri Lankan, 38–39; Tamil, 23–24, 27, 44, 49–51, 101, 116, 123, 125–27, 136; and tradition, 27–28, 62, 135; transnational, 21, 26, 30, 44–45; understanding, 61–65; Western, 27, 45, 115, 121

dance: drama format, 86–89; education, 19–20, 52, 58–63; and ethnicity, 7–9, 109; Kalakshetra, 29–36; as meaningful, 101–7; multiculturalism, 98–101; as norm for girls of status, 22–24, 28–29; as spiritual practice, 94; and Tamil culture, 125–27; teaching of, 63–76; technique and vocabulary, 9–14; during war, 2–3, 80, 136–37. *See also* bharata natyam; Kandyan dance

"The Dancer" (commercial), 129–31

Daniel, Smriti, 138

David, Ann, 144n12

De Alwis, Malathi, 30, 33, 143n11

demands of research, 45, 147n4

De Mel, Neloufer, 8, 91

democracy, 56, 138

Department of Education, 41, 61

Desai, Radhika, 54–55

De Silva, Chandra Richard, 55–56

de Silva, Daya, 55–56

Destradi, Sandra, 151n5

devadasis (temple performers): Ancukam, 23–25, 27–29, 31, 40; and arangetram, 49, 94; bharata natyam, 12; in film, 113, 144n6; *nattuvanars*, 31, 145n7; recontextualization, 43–44; religious reform movement, 22–23; *sadir*, 22, 32, 121; tradition, 12, 27–28, 86; vulgarity, 31–32

developmental nationalism, 74–75

development work, 5, 7, 12, 24, 52–55, 60, 131, 136–37

Devini (teacher), 71

DeVotta, Neil, 4

Dharmapala, Angarika, 25, 32, 41, 45

dialogical tensions, 29–30

politics: and Bhabha, 50–51; dance,
13–14, 134; equality, 74–75; identity,
4–5, 41–42; and Indian Tamils, 40–42;
neoliberalism, 53–55; in performance,
106–7; politicization of movement,
2–3, 8–9; radical, 8, 140; and restriction
of identity, 125–26; and ritual, 28; and
Tamil culture, 82, 87; and Tamil identity, 125–26; transnational, 45–46
polyandry, 33
Ponnambalam, G. G., 40
popular culture, 108, 112, 115, 121
postcolonial, 5, 7, 12, 39, 50, 56, 101, 106,
121, 126. *See also* colonialism
postwar Sri Lanka, 132–40
Prabhakaran (LTTE leader), 131
The Production of Space (Lefebvre), 79–80
professional opportunities, 58, 68–69, 71
pronunciation, 99
Prothero, Stephen, 25–26
public education and aesthetics education, 52–53, 55–73, 74–75, 145n1
public spaces, 96, 97, 102, 105
public sphere, 31–32
puja (ritual blessing), 94–95

racial labels, 4. *See also* difference
radical politics, 8, 140
Rajapaksa, Mahinda, 134
Rajasingham-Senanayake, Darini, 54
Rambukwella, Keheliya, 89
Rangana (teacher), 29–31, 33, 35–36, 62
rationale for conflict, 12–13
reconciliations, 9, 131, 138
reconstruction, 12, 30, 35–36, 52, 93
recontextualization of Buddhist practices,
7, 13, 43, 143n5, 146n5
Reed, Susan, 13, 43, 59–60, 67, 70–72, 121,
122, 146n5, 146n14
reform. *See* social reform movement
refugees, 6, 141. *See also* diaspora
regional identification, 4, 33–34
rehabilitation, 130–31, 137–38
rejection, 4, 13, 126, 136, 140–41

religion: bharata natyam, 88, 98; devadasis, 22–23, 28, 31; and identity, 3, 33–35,
98; and language, 98, 100, 104–5; multiculturalism, 104; rationale for conflict,
12–13; religious enunciations, 98; text
vs., 25–26. *See also* Hinduism
renaming and resituating, 30
repertoire, 35, 80, 85–87, 88, 95, 101–4,
146nn10–11
repetitive practices, 126
repopulation, 30
representation: and choreography, 80; of
difference, 131, 136–37; in *Draupadhi Sabatham*, 84; economics, 54; ethnic, 98;
and fixity, 46; minority, 3–5, 42, 62–63,
98, 136–37, 139; multiculturalism, 99;
Phelan on, 126; Tamilness, 75, 139;
"The Dancer" billboard, 129–31; in *Title
Dance*, 109, 115–16, 123, 126–27; visual,
116; women, 116
represented dance. *See* bharata natyam
restoration, 30
restriction of Tamilness, 125–26
retaliation, 92
retention, 125–26
revival, 12–13, 24–25, 30–31, 35, 53, 86–87,
95, 101, 104
rhetorical strategies, 23–25
Rhythm of Life (Kalalaya), 39
riots, 4, 34, 47–49
ritual, 23, 25–26, 28, 43, 94–95
Roberts, Michael, 41
Rogers, John, 33, 35–36, 41
rural schools, 57
Ruwanpura, Kanchana, 86

sabdam (item in repertoire), 68, 146n11
sacralization of sex, 33
sadir (dance practice), 22, 31–32, 98, 121
Saiva Mangaiyar Kalagam, 26–28, 32
Saiva religious reform movement, 22–23
Sakthi (Kalalaya), 39
Salcedo, Doris, 14
sameness, 4, 105, 123, 126

Sanchari Bhava, 146n4

Sangam literature, 49–50

sangha (Buddhist monastic community), 26

Sansuka (producer), 111–12, 116, 118–21, 123

sari traditional styles, 93, 150n1

Savigliano, Marta, 9

scenario concept, 102–3

Scott, Anna, 9

secondary education, 56

segregation, 5–6, 59, 67–68, 74, 100–101, 105, 134

separatism, 4, 6, 8–9, 21, 82. *See also* Liberation Tigers

settler colonialism, 140

sexuality, 33, 118, 121, 130

shadow diaspora, 150n3

Shakthi Superstar (television series), 108, 110–12, 115, 118–23, 125–27, 149n4

Shakthi TV, 81–82, 110

Shankar, Uday, 39

Shankari (choreographer), 92–95, 98–101, 103, 105

Shanti (*Peace*), 92–106

shanti (Sanskrit term), 98, 105

Sharmini (dancer), 117

shlokas (verses), 66, 69, 77, 146n7, 147n3

Sillapathikaram, 44, 49

Silva, Neluka, 3

Sinhala-Only Act, 43–44, 59, 63, 145n2

Sinhalas: bharata natyam, 67–68, 73; culture, 100, 145n3; diaspora, 12; education, 55–59, 67–68; ethnicity, 3–5; government, 2, 137; identity, 47, 98; institutional multiculturalism, 100; Kandyan dance, 2, 13–14, 43, 139; language, 3–5, 43–44, 59, 61, 63, 95–96, 104, 132–33, 145nn2–3; lyrics, 96, 99, 132–33; minority, 98; music, 60; nationalism, 7, 13, 25, 41, 49, 92; passing as, 99–100; polyandry, 33; *Title Dance*, 115, 126–27; violence, 47–48

Sirasa Superstar (television series), 110

SLFP (Sri Lankan Freedom Party), 58–59, 145n2

social categories, 34, 36, 42

social reform movement, 22–29, 32, 39, 41, 44, 50

sociology of culture, 14

sollukattu (verbal syllables), 69

Soneji, Davesh, 22–23, 28

Sonia (teacher), 66–72, 112

South Asian diaspora, 13–14, 94

South Asian films, 114, 126–27

Spencer, Jonathan, 57–58

spirituality, 34–35, 94, 98

Sri Lanka: army, 64, 136; bharata natyam, 98; Bring Back the Child campaign, 128–31; certifications, 70–71; colonization, 143n8; conflict, 82, 87, 92; culture, 38–39; education, 55–60; ethnicity, 7–9; ethnography, 10–14; government, 2, 5, 11–12, 52, 100, 131–32, 134, 137–38, 151nn5–6; hybridity of, 45; identity, 35–36; and India, 134, 150n4; indigeneity, 41–42; innovation in dance, 106; militarism, 3–6; national dance, 37–39, 43–44; nationalisms, 131; North American Academy, 140–41; policies, 52–53; postwar, 132–40; public education, 52–53, 55–73, 74–75; riots, 47; Tamils, 3, 29–30, 42–44, 146n14, 149n3; teaching in, 66–71; women, 30, 32–33. *See also* civil war; Colombo

Sri Lankan Freedom Party (SLFP), 58–59, 145n2

sringara (erotic) elements in song, 32

Srinivasan, Amit, 12

Srinivasan, P., 147n5

Sruti (magazine), 32

standardization, 58, 68

state: antistate insurrections, 57–58; and dance, 75; divestment, 75; employment, 59, 75; and local relationships, 21; multiculturalism, 51, 75; one culture notion, 53; pogroms, 11; postcolonial, 56; rehabilitation programs, 130, 137–38;

sanctioned histories, 75; security, 137; sponsored performance, 60, 74; statelessness, 40–41, 45, 49
structural adjustment programs, 74
Sunday Observer (newspaper), 34
swabhasha (local languages), 67
Swedish International Development Agency, 60, 70
symbolic value, 8, 136
symbols of culture, 51, 62

tala (rhythmic cycle), 66, 146n6
Tamil Maanavar Sangam (Tamil Students Union of the Ladies' College), 81
Tamil Maanavar Sangham (Tamil Students Union event), 94
Tamil Makkal Viduthalai Pulikal, 150n2
Tamils: anti-Tamil riots, 47–49; and bharata natyam, 49–51, 62, 65, 72, 75, 125–26, 139–40, 144n12; bodies, 2, 36, 65, 72, 75, 78, 97, 102, 105, 115, 120, 130; Bring Back the Child campaign, 130–31; Christian, 3, 25–27; cinema, 147n6; civil war, 97, 123–24, 132–33, 136–37, 150n3; community, 41; culture, 23–24, 27, 44, 49–51, 101, 116, 123, 125–27, 136; dancers and dance teachers, 111–15; diaspora, 6, 11–12, 92, 134, 141, 144n12; *Draupadhi Sabatham*, 81–92, 102; ethnicity, 3–6, 36; film, 113; gatherings, 89; Hindu, 3; identity, 27, 99, 115, 125, 143n6, 144n12; and India, 146n14; Indian, 40–42; institutional multiculturalism, 100; Jaffna, 144n5; and Kandyan dance, 72, 122; language, 3–5, 27, 67–68, 81–83, 86–87, 104, 127, 133, 145n3, 146n14; lyrics, 95–96, 132; Malaiyaha, 4, 39–40, 45; militarized areas, 139; nationalism, 44, 49–51; people, 123–24; performances, 133; politics, 40–42, 82, 87, 125–26; public education, 52–53, 55–73, 74–75; resistance movements, 57–58; retaliation, 92; revival, 145–46n3; separatists, 2; Sinhala Buddhist, 2; social reform, 24–25; Sri Lankan, 3, 29–30, 42–44, 146n14, 149n3; students, 67; Tamilness, 20, 28, 36, 50–51, 65, 75, 78, 89, 115, 123, 125–26, 131, 136, 139; teachers, 126; *Title Dance*, 108–27; tradition, 42, 44, 87; women, 24, 26–29, 30, 92–93. *See also* Liberation Tigers of Tamil Eelam

Tamil Students Union of the Ladies' College (Tamil Maanavar Sangam), 81, 85–87, 89
Tamil Tigers. *See* Liberation Tigers of Tamil Eelam
Tamil Women's Union, 39
"Tamizh Mozhi Vaazhttu" (Bharati), 81, 87
ta tai tai ta (bharata grouping), 68
tatta (adavus), 68, 146n9
tat tai tam (*korvai*) (bharata grouping), 68
Taylor, Diana, 85, 87, 101–3, 107
Taylor, Julie, 14
Tenekoon, Serena, 47
texts *vs.* religious practices, 25–26, 85–89, 104
Thai Pongal festival, 64
theory knowledge, 69
Theravada Buddhism, 3
Theva Gnana Nadanam ("Ceylon Causerie"), 39
Thimitakata (bharata natyam dance competition television series), 110–11
Thiranagama, Sharika, 3–4, 79–80, 97, 150n3
Thirana (producer), 111–12, 116–21, 123
Thirteenth Amendment, Sri Lankan Constitution, 104
Thiruchandran, Selvy, 8, 24
Title Dance: beginnings of, 109–16; costuming, 115–24; dismissal of dancing woman, 149n7; overview, 108–9; postconcert reflections, 124–27; profitability, 150n10
tradition: bharata natyam, 3, 20, 78, 88, 113, 120–21; and culture, 27–28, 135; dance as, 102; *devadasis*, 12, 27–28, 86;

and dialogical tensions, 29–30; and
identity, 62; Indian, 39; Kandyan dance,
122, 146n5; multiculturalism, 94–95; and
nationalisms, 106; performances, 103–7,
122; Sri Lankan, 56; Tamil, 42, 44, 87
transnational and translational, 14, 21, 26–
28, 29–30, 45–46, 51, 126–27, 136, 139–40

UK Department for International Devel-
opment, 129
UNESCO (United Nations Educational,
Scientific, and Cultural Organization),
52–53, 56, 59–60
UNHRC (United Nations Human Rights
Council), 151n5
UNICEF (United Nations International
Children's Emergency Fund), 128–30
uniqueness, 106
United National Party (UNP), 58
United Nations, 137–38
United Nations Educational, Scientific,
and Cultural Organization (UNESCO),
52–53, 56, 59–60
United Nations Human Rights Council
(UNHRC), 151n5
United Nations International Children's
Emergency Fund (UNICEF), 128–30
universal adult franchise, 55
universality, of bharata natyam, 34–35,
98, 103
University of Jaffna, 138–39
University of Visual and Performing Arts,
61
Unmarked (Phelan), 126
UNP (United National Party), 58
uprisings, 48, 57–58
urban schools, 57
Uruttirakanikaiyar (Ancukam), 23
Uyangoda, Jeyadeva, 137

"Vakratunda Mahakaya," 77
vannam (form of dance), 143n5
Vellalar, 22–24
vernacular schools, 55–56

Vilzha, Pavala, 147n9
violence, 5, 45–49, 58, 78–79, 85–86, 89,
91, 99, 130, 135–39, 143–44n11. *See also*
civil war
virali and viral vallabam kattum (artists
who perform hand gestures), 49–50
visual representations. *See* costuming
Visweswaran, Kamala, 147n4
vocational-oriented educational curricu-
lums, 58
vulgarity, 31–33

Wanasinghe, Jayampati, 57
Wanniya Laeto, 3, 23, 41–42
Wayland, Sarah, 6
Wellawatte neighborhood, 47, 110, 116,
124, 135–36
West/Western: culture, 27, 45, 115, 121;
dance, 38, 112; feminism, 121; intervention, 141; music, 60; Orientalism, 26;
powers, 137
white van syndrome, 89, 124
Wickremasinghe, Nira, 104
Williams, Raymond, 14
Wilson, A. Jeyaratnam, 4
Winslow, Deborah, 149n3
women: agency, 137; bodies, 12, 24, 71–72,
75–76, 86, 89–91, 109, 114, 117–18, 121;
Buddhism, 25; caste and class, 23–24;
ethnography, 7–8; Kalakshetra form,
30; Kandyan dance, 13; organizational
work, 27–28; public sphere, 32; representation, 116; Tamil, 24, 26–29, 30,
92–93; as victims, 148n14; womanhood,
29, 30, 121
*Women and the Nation's Narrative: Gender
and Nationalism in Twentieth Century Sri
Lanka* (De Mel), 91
Woost, Michael D., 149n3

Yamini (choreographer), 108, 112, 116,
118–19, 149n5
Yogendran (teacher), 88, 94, 148n17
youth-led antistate insurrections, 57–58

About the Author

Ahalya Satkunaratnam is a choreographer, dancer, and dance scholar who lives and works on the unceded and traditional territories of the Tseil-Watuth, Musqueum, and Sqaumish Nations. She joined the faculty of Quest University Canada in 2014. There she teaches courses in performing arts, women's and gender studies, and cultural studies. Her articles have appeared in *Dance Research Journal*, *SAMAR: South Asian Magazine for Action and Reflection*, and *Options Magazine*, as well as in other edited collections. Her choreographic works have been performed in Sri Lanka, the United States, and Canada.